Entebbe Unveiled: The Israeli Military's Heroic Rescue Mission

Copyright Page

TITLE: Entebbe Unveiled: The Israeli Military's Heroic Rescue Mission

1ST Edition

Table of Contents

Entebbe Unveiled: The Israeli Military's Heroic Rescue Mission

By Roberto Miguel Rodriguez

Introduction

Each chapter of "Entebbe Unveiled: The Israeli Military's Heroic Rescue Mission" provides a comprehensive exploration of the respective topic, offering insights, analysis, and historical context for diplomats and historians interested in understanding the complexities of the Entebbe rescue mission and its wide-ranging impact.

"The Role of the Israeli Military in the Rescue Mission at Entebbe" delves into the meticulous planning and execution of the daring operation by the Israeli Defense Forces (IDF). It examines the military strategies employed, the challenges faced, and the bravery displayed by the Israeli soldiers who risked their lives to save their countrymen.

"The Personal Stories and Experiences of the Israeli Passengers During Their Captivity" brings to light the harrowing tales of the hostages who endured days of captivity under the threat of violence. Through interviews and firsthand accounts, this chapter paints a vivid picture of their resilience, fear, and ultimate liberation.

"The Diplomatic Efforts and Negotiations Behind the Scenes to Secure the Release of the Hostages" uncovers the intricate negotiations and diplomatic maneuvers that took place to secure the safe return of the hostages. It sheds light on the delicate balance of power and the international collaboration necessary to navigate the complex political landscape surrounding the hijacking.

"The Impact of the Entebbe Rescue Mission on Israeli Society and National Identity" explores how the successful rescue operation became a defining moment in Israeli history, bolstering national pride and solidarity. It analyzes the long-lasting effects of the mission on Israeli society, military doctrine, and the perception of Israel on the global stage.

"The Historical Context and Geopolitical Implications of the Hijacking and Rescue Operation" provides a historical backdrop, examining the geopolitical factors that led to the hijacking and the subsequent rescue mission. It analyzes the regional tensions, the Cold War dynamics, and the strategic implications of the operation on the Middle East.

"The Role of Mossad (Israeli Intelligence Agency) in Gathering Information and Planning the Rescue Mission" delves into the intelligence-gathering operations conducted by Mossad, highlighting their crucial role in providing critical information for the successful execution of the rescue mission.

"The Aftermath of the Entebbe Rescue Mission and Its Long-Term Effects on Counterterrorism Strategies" explores how the Entebbe operation reshaped the global understanding of counterterrorism. It examines the lessons learned, the impact on international security measures, and the evolution of counterterrorism strategies in the decades that followed.

"The Role of International Support and Cooperation in the Success of the Rescue Mission" highlights the support and cooperation extended by various governments and organizations, showcasing the significance of international solidarity in the success of the rescue mission.

"The Media Coverage and Public Perception of the Entebbe Hijacking and Subsequent Rescue" analyzes the media's role in shaping public opinion and disseminating information about the hijacking and the subsequent rescue operation. It examines the coverage, controversies, and the impact on public perception of the events.

"The Stories of the Ugandan Hostages and Their Perspective on the Events at Entebbe" sheds light on the experiences and perspectives of the Ugandan hostages, often overlooked in the narrative. By giving voice to their stories, this chapter offers a comprehensive understanding of the events from multiple viewpoints.

"Entebbe Unveiled: The Israeli Military's Heroic Rescue Mission" is an invaluable resource for diplomats and historians seeking a comprehensive exploration of the Entebbe rescue mission and its profound impact on global politics, counterterrorism strategies, and national identities.

Chapter 1: The Role of the Israeli Military in the Rescue Mission at Entebbe

The Hijacking of Air France Flight 139

The hijacking of Air France Flight 139 on June 27, 1976, marked a pivotal moment in the history of counterterrorism and the Israeli military. This subchapter delves into the captivating and harrowing events that unfolded during the hijacking and subsequent rescue mission at Entebbe. Addressed to diplomats and historians, it offers a comprehensive examination of the various aspects surrounding this audacious operation.

The role of the Israeli military in the rescue mission at Entebbe is a central theme in this subchapter. It explores the meticulous planning, precise execution, and the bravery displayed by the elite Israeli commandos who risked their lives in the daring operation. Their strategic brilliance and unwavering determination to bring their countrymen home safely reflect the indomitable spirit of the Israeli armed forces.

Additionally, this subchapter highlights the personal stories and experiences of the Israeli passengers during their captivity. Through interviews and firsthand accounts, readers gain insight into the physical and emotional challenges faced by these innocent civilians as they endured days of uncertainty and fear under the watchful eyes of their captors.

The diplomatic efforts and negotiations behind the scenes to secure the release of the hostages are also examined. This includes the role played by international actors and the delicate balance between diplomacy and the use of military force in resolving the crisis. The subchapter sheds light on the intricate web of negotiations that unfolded, ultimately leading to the success of the rescue mission.

Furthermore, the subchapter explores the impact of the Entebbe rescue mission on Israeli society and national identity. It analyzes how the successful operation bolstered national pride and served as a symbol of Israel's resolve to protect its citizens against terrorism. The subchapter also delves into the historical context and geopolitical implications of the hijacking and rescue operation, examining how it shaped regional dynamics and international relations.

The role of Mossad, the Israeli intelligence agency, in gathering information and planning the rescue mission is another crucial aspect covered in this subchapter. It explores the agency's covert operations and intelligence-gathering methods, underscoring their instrumental role in the mission's success.

Additionally, the subchapter delves into the aftermath of the Entebbe rescue mission and its long-term effects on counterterrorism strategies. It examines how this operation influenced the development of international counterterrorism efforts and shaped the way nations respond to similar crises.

The subchapter also explores the role of international support and cooperation in the success of the rescue mission. It highlights the alliances forged and the assistance provided by various countries, demonstrating the significance of international collaboration in combating terrorism.

Moreover, this subchapter analyzes the media coverage and public perception of the Entebbe hijacking and subsequent rescue. It assesses the portrayal of the events in the media and the impact it had on public opinion both domestically and internationally.

Lastly, to provide a comprehensive account of the events at Entebbe, the subchapter delves into the stories of the Ugandan hostages and their perspective on the events. By examining their experiences and narratives, readers gain a deeper understanding of the complexities and human toll of this tragic event.

In conclusion, this subchapter offers a multifaceted exploration of the hijacking of Air France Flight 139 and the subsequent rescue mission at Entebbe. Through its comprehensive examination of the Israeli military's role, personal stories, diplomatic efforts, historical context, and geopolitical implications, it provides diplomats and historians with a thorough understanding of this watershed moment in counterterrorism history.

The Decision to Mount a Rescue Operation

In the subchapter titled "The Decision to Mount a Rescue Operation" in the book "Entebbe Unveiled: The Israeli Military's Heroic Rescue Mission," we delve into the pivotal moment when the Israeli military made the courageous choice to embark on a daring rescue mission at Entebbe. This chapter aims to captivate the attention of diplomats and historians, shedding light on the multifaceted aspects surrounding this remarkable event.

The role of the Israeli military in the rescue mission at Entebbe is examined, highlighting the meticulous planning, coordination, and execution of the operation. The personal stories and experiences of the Israeli passengers during their captivity provide a poignant and intimate account of the harrowing ordeal they endured.

Furthermore, the diplomatic efforts and negotiations behind the scenes to secure the release of the hostages are explored, emphasizing the delicate balance between diplomacy and military action. This section provides insight into the intricate web of negotiations and the challenges faced by the Israeli government.

We also delve into the impact of the Entebbe rescue mission on Israeli society and national identity. This historic event galvanized the nation, fostering a sense of unity, pride, and resilience in the face of adversity. The chapter delves into the cultural and psychological significance of the rescue operation, illustrating how it became a defining moment in Israeli history.

The historical context and geopolitical implications of the hijacking and rescue operation are examined, shedding light on the intricacies of Middle Eastern politics during that era. The role of Mossad, the Israeli intelligence agency, in gathering information and planning the rescue mission, is also explored, showcasing their expertise and resourcefulness.

The aftermath of the Entebbe rescue mission and its long-term effects on counterterrorism strategies are discussed, unveiling its influence on global security measures. The chapter also highlights the role of international support and cooperation in the success of the rescue mission, underscoring the significance of collaborative efforts in combating terrorism.

Moreover, the media coverage and public perception of the Entebbe hijacking and subsequent rescue are analyzed, offering an insight into how the event was portrayed globally. Additionally, the chapter delves into the stories of the Ugandan hostages and their perspective on the events at Entebbe, providing a comprehensive view of the entire ordeal.

In conclusion, this subchapter serves as a comprehensive exploration of the decision-making process behind the Entebbe rescue operation. It delves into the various aspects surrounding the event, catering to the interests of diplomats and historians alike, while providing a gripping account of this extraordinary mission.

Operation Thunderbolt: Planning and Preparation

Operation Thunderbolt, the daring Israeli military rescue mission at Entebbe, stands as a testament to the ingenuity, bravery, and unwavering commitment of the Israeli military. In this subchapter, we delve into the meticulous planning and preparation that went into executing this extraordinary operation.

At the heart of Operation Thunderbolt was the Israeli military's resolve to save their fellow citizens held captive by terrorists. The planning process began immediately after the Air France plane was hijacked and diverted to Entebbe Airport in Uganda. The Israeli military, renowned for its swift and decisive action, understood the urgency of the situation and wasted no time in formulating a rescue plan.

Central to the success of Operation Thunderbolt was the role of the Mossad, the Israeli intelligence agency. The Mossad played a crucial role in gathering vital information about the hijackers, their demands, and the layout of the airport. This intelligence formed the basis for the meticulous planning of the rescue mission, ensuring that every possible scenario was anticipated and accounted for.

The planning team, led by Colonel Yonatan Netanyahu, meticulously studied the terrain, the airport layout, and the terrorists' movements. They devised a plan that involved a lightning-fast assault by Israeli commandos who would surprise the hijackers, neutralize their defenses, and rescue the hostages. The team also meticulously prepared for contingencies, such as the potential involvement of Ugandan forces.

Simultaneously, behind the scenes, diplomats and negotiators worked tirelessly to secure the release of the hostages. These efforts involved delicate negotiations with the Ugandan government and other international actors. The diplomatic maneuvering was crucial in buying time for the Israeli military to plan and execute the rescue operation.

The impact of the Entebbe rescue mission on Israeli society and national identity cannot be overstated. It was a moment of national unity and pride, demonstrating Israel's unwavering commitment to protecting its citizens. The successful rescue mission served as a turning point in the fight against terrorism and solidified Israel's reputation as a nation that would stop at nothing to protect its people.

The international support and cooperation received by Israel were instrumental in the success of Operation Thunderbolt. Several countries, including the United States, provided crucial logistical and intelligence support, further underscoring the global battle against terrorism.

As the rescue mission unfolded, the media coverage and public perception of the Entebbe hijacking and subsequent rescue were overwhelmingly positive. The world witnessed the Israeli military's audacity and precision, which captivated diplomats and historians alike. The stories of the Israeli passengers during their captivity and the perspective of the Ugandan hostages further shed light on the human aspect of this remarkable event.

The aftermath of the Entebbe rescue mission had profound and lasting effects on counterterrorism strategies worldwide. Governments and security agencies around the globe studied and drew inspiration from the Israeli military's success in planning and executing a complex operation against formidable odds.

In conclusion, Operation Thunderbolt exemplified the Israeli military's unparalleled planning and preparation, highlighting the role of the Mossad, the diplomatic efforts, and the international support that contributed to its success. The Entebbe rescue mission not only left an indelible mark on Israeli society but also reshaped global perceptions of counterterrorism and forever altered the course of history.

The Israeli Defense Forces' Execution of the Rescue Mission

The daring rescue mission at Entebbe, carried out by the Israeli Defense Forces (IDF), stands as a testament to their unwavering commitment to protecting their citizens and their ability to execute complex military operations. This subchapter delves into the meticulous planning and execution of the mission, highlighting the exceptional skills and bravery of the IDF.

The rescue operation was a meticulously planned and flawlessly executed mission that involved a range of military tactics, including covert operations, intelligence gathering, and precision airstrikes. The IDF utilized their expertise in special forces operations, employing elite commando units such as the Sayeret Matkal to infiltrate Entebbe Airport undetected.

The personal stories and experiences of the Israeli passengers during their captivity are an integral part of this subchapter. Through interviews and firsthand accounts, we gain a deep understanding of the psychological toll and resilience displayed by the hostages. Their unwavering hope and determination to survive, despite the constant threat of violence, are truly inspiring.

Behind the scenes, diplomatic efforts and negotiations played a crucial role in securing the release of the hostages. This subchapter sheds light on the tireless work of Israeli diplomats and the delicate balance they maintained in navigating international politics. Their negotiations with various governments and the strategic alliances forged behind closed doors ultimately paved the way for the successful rescue.

The impact of the Entebbe rescue mission on Israeli society and national identity cannot be overstated. This subchapter examines how the mission galvanized the nation, instilling a sense of pride and unity among its people. The rescue became a defining moment in Israel's history, solidifying its reputation as a formidable force in the face of terrorism.

To understand the historical context and geopolitical implications of the hijacking and rescue operation, this subchapter delves into the underlying factors that led to the crisis. It explores the rise of international terrorism and the growing threat faced by countries worldwide. The Entebbe rescue mission emerged as a pivotal event, shaping counterterrorism strategies for years to come.

The role of Mossad, the Israeli intelligence agency, in gathering information and planning the rescue mission is another key aspect covered in this subchapter. Mossad's meticulous intelligence gathering and covert operations laid the groundwork for the successful execution of the mission. Their expertise and unwavering dedication to protecting Israeli citizens played a pivotal role in the operation's success.

The aftermath of the Entebbe rescue mission and its long-term effects on counterterrorism strategies are also explored in this subchapter. It analyzes how the operation influenced international approaches to combating terrorism and provided valuable lessons for future operations.

The role of international support and cooperation in the success of the rescue mission is another crucial aspect covered in this subchapter. It delves into the alliances formed with various countries and the critical support they provided, underscoring the significance of international solidarity in combating terrorism.

The media coverage and public perception of the Entebbe hijacking and subsequent rescue are also examined. This subchapter highlights the global attention the crisis garnered and the impact it had on public opinion, shedding light on the media's portrayal of the event.

Finally, the subchapter delves into the stories of the Ugandan hostages, offering their perspective on the events at Entebbe. Their experiences provide a unique insight into the tragedy and highlight the lasting impact it had on their lives.

In conclusion, this subchapter provides a comprehensive examination of the Israeli Defense Forces' execution of the rescue mission at Entebbe. It explores the multifaceted aspects of the operation, from the military tactics employed to the diplomatic efforts behind the scenes. By delving into personal stories, diplomatic negotiations, historical context, and geopolitical implications, this subchapter offers a comprehensive understanding of the heroic rescue mission and its far-reaching effects.

The Successful Outcome and Heroes of Entebbe

The Entebbe rescue mission stands as a shining testament to the unwavering determination and heroism of the Israeli military. This subchapter delves into the successful outcome of the mission and pays tribute to the brave individuals who risked their lives to save others.

The Israeli military's role in the rescue mission at Entebbe was nothing short of extraordinary. Against all odds, a team of elite commandos executed a daring operation that resulted in the liberation of over 100 hostages held captive by terrorists. Their meticulous planning, audacious execution, and unwavering commitment to the mission's success have since become legendary.

Entebbe Unveiled also sheds light on the personal stories and experiences of the Israeli passengers during their harrowing captivity. Through interviews and firsthand accounts, readers gain insight into the psychological and emotional toll endured by these individuals, as well as their resilience and unwavering hope for liberation.

Behind the scenes, diplomatic efforts and negotiations were underway to secure the release of the hostages. This subchapter explores the intricate web of international diplomacy that played a crucial role in the success of the mission. It highlights the tireless efforts of diplomats and negotiators who worked around the clock to ensure a peaceful resolution and the safe return of the hostages.

The impact of the Entebbe rescue mission on Israeli society and national identity is also examined in this subchapter. The audacious operation galvanized the Israeli people, instilling a renewed sense of national pride and unity. It became a defining moment in the nation's history, reaffirming its commitment to protect its citizens against all threats.

Entebbe Unveiled also delves into the historical context and geopolitical implications of the hijacking and rescue operation. It explores the factors that led to the hijacking, the motivations of the terrorists, and the broader implications for international security.

Integral to the success of the mission was the role of Mossad, the Israeli intelligence agency. The subchapter provides an in-depth look at Mossad's pivotal role in gathering critical information, planning the rescue mission, and ensuring its seamless execution.

The aftermath of the Entebbe rescue mission and its long-term effects on counterterrorism strategies are also explored. The mission served as a blueprint for future operations, revolutionizing the way counterterrorism efforts were approached worldwide.

The subchapter also highlights the importance of international support and cooperation in the mission's success. It acknowledges the contributions made by various nations and their intelligence agencies, underscoring the significance of collaboration in combating terrorism.

The media coverage and public perception of the Entebbe hijacking and subsequent rescue are also examined. This section provides an analysis of how the events unfolded in the media and the impact it had on shaping public opinion and understanding of the incident.

Lastly, Entebbe Unveiled offers a glimpse into the stories of the Ugandan hostages and their perspective on the events at Entebbe. Their experiences and insights provide a unique and often overlooked dimension to the narrative, giving voice to those who endured unimaginable trauma.

In conclusion, this subchapter of Entebbe Unveiled provides a comprehensive account of the successful outcome and the heroes of Entebbe. It explores the multifaceted aspects of the rescue mission, shedding light on the Israeli military's role, the personal stories of the hostages, the diplomatic efforts, the historical context, and the long-term implications. It is a testament to the indomitable spirit of those involved and a tribute to their unwavering commitment to justice and freedom.

Chapter 2: The Personal Stories and Experiences of the Israeli Passengers during their Captivity

The Initial Shock and Fear

In the summer of 1976, the world watched in horror as an Air France plane was hijacked and diverted to Entebbe, Uganda. This daring act of terrorism sent shockwaves across the globe, leaving the Israeli passengers on board in a state of utter fear and uncertainty. As the hostages were separated from the rest of the passengers and held captive by the terrorists, their lives hung in the balance.

For the Israeli military, the news of the hijacking hit home hard. With their own citizens in grave danger, they knew they had to act swiftly and decisively. The initial shock turned into a fierce determination to bring their people home safely, no matter the cost.

Meanwhile, the Israeli passengers endured unimaginable hardships during their captivity. Forced to live in cramped conditions, surrounded by armed guards, they grappled with fear and despair. However, amidst the darkness, stories of resilience and courage emerged. Each hostage had their own personal tale of survival, as they drew strength from one another and clung onto the hope of rescue.

Behind the scenes, diplomatic efforts and negotiations were underway to secure the release of the hostages. Israeli officials worked tirelessly to rally international support, seeking any avenue that could lead to a peaceful resolution. The world watched as diplomats navigated delicate negotiations, hoping for a breakthrough that would bring an end to this harrowing ordeal.

The Entebbe rescue mission had far-reaching implications for Israeli society and its national identity. The successful operation not only showcased the unwavering commitment of the Israeli military to protect its citizens but also bolstered the nation's confidence in its ability to combat terrorism. It became a defining moment in Israel's history, a symbol of its resilience and determination in the face of adversity.

The rescue operation also had significant geopolitical implications. It highlighted the lengths to which Israel would go to protect its people, sending a clear message to its enemies. Moreover, the role of Mossad, Israel's renowned intelligence agency, in gathering crucial information and planning the rescue mission, showcased their expertise and resourcefulness in the field of counterterrorism.

As the dust settled, the aftermath of the Entebbe rescue mission reverberated across the globe. It had a lasting impact on counterterrorism strategies, shaping the way nations approached hostage situations. The international support and cooperation that aided the success of the mission highlighted the importance of global unity in combating terrorism.

The media coverage and public perception of the Entebbe hijacking and subsequent rescue played a significant role in shaping public opinion. The stories of bravery and heroism that emerged from the crisis captivated the world, portraying the Israeli military as a force to be reckoned with.

While much attention was given to the Israeli passengers, the stories of the Ugandan hostages cannot be overlooked. Their perspective on the events at Entebbe offers a unique insight into the impact of the hijacking on their lives and their country.

In "Entebbe Unveiled: The Israeli Military's Heroic Rescue Mission," diplomats and historians will find a comprehensive exploration of these various aspects, shedding light on the role of the Israeli military, the personal stories of the hostages, the diplomatic efforts behind the scenes, the geopolitical implications, the role of Mossad, and the long-term effects of the rescue mission. This book offers a rich tapestry of narratives, providing a deep understanding of one of the most remarkable rescue missions in history.

Living Conditions and Psychological Impact

During their captivity at Entebbe, the Israeli passengers endured extremely challenging living conditions that had a profound psychological impact on them. The hostages were held in a cramped room with minimal amenities, including inadequate food and water supplies. The lack of proper sanitation facilities and limited access to medical care further exacerbated their already dire circumstances.

The psychological toll of the hostages' captivity cannot be overstated. They were subjected to constant threats and intimidation by their captors, who were armed and unpredictable. The Israeli passengers lived in a perpetual state of fear and uncertainty, not knowing whether they would survive the ordeal or ever be reunited with their loved ones.

The hostages developed various coping mechanisms to endure their captivity. They formed close bonds with one another, providing support and comfort in a time of extreme distress. They found solace in their shared experiences and relied on each other for emotional support.

The prolonged captivity took a toll on the mental well-being of the hostages. Many experienced symptoms of post-traumatic stress disorder (PTSD) once they were released. Flashbacks, nightmares, and anxiety became a part of their daily lives as they struggled to come to terms with the trauma they had endured.

The psychological impact of the Entebbe rescue mission extended beyond the hostages themselves. Israeli society was deeply affected by the events at Entebbe, with the nation rallying behind the hostages and their families. The successful rescue mission became a symbol of Israeli resilience and determination in the face of terrorism.

Moreover, the Entebbe rescue mission had significant geopolitical implications. It demonstrated Israel's unwavering commitment to the safety and security of its citizens, sending a strong message to terrorist organizations worldwide. The mission also showcased the effectiveness of Israeli intelligence and military capabilities, bolstering the country's international reputation.

The media coverage of the Entebbe hijacking and subsequent rescue played a crucial role in shaping public perception. The world watched in awe as Israeli commandos carried out a daring operation thousands of miles from home. The coverage highlighted the bravery and heroism of the Israeli military, further solidifying their status as national heroes.

While much attention has been given to the Israeli passengers, it is important to also consider the stories and perspectives of the Ugandan hostages. Their lives were forever changed by the events at Entebbe, and their experiences offer valuable insights into the complexities of the situation.

In conclusion, the living conditions endured by the Israeli passengers during their captivity at Entebbe had a profound psychological impact on them. The successful rescue mission not only had significant implications for Israeli society and national identity but also shed light on the historical context and geopolitical implications of the hijacking. The role of Mossad in gathering information and planning the rescue mission, as well as the international support and cooperation, were instrumental in its success. The aftermath of the Entebbe rescue mission and its long-term effects on counterterrorism strategies cannot be understated. Ultimately, the stories of the hostages from both sides provide a comprehensive understanding of the events at Entebbe.

Acts of Resistance and Solidarity

One of the most remarkable aspects of the Entebbe rescue mission was the unwavering acts of resistance and solidarity displayed by both the Israeli hostages and the Israeli military. These acts not only demonstrated the indomitable spirit of the Israeli people, but also showcased their determination to combat terrorism and protect their fellow citizens.

Throughout their captivity, the Israeli passengers exhibited immense courage and resilience. Despite being held hostage by terrorists, they refused to succumb to fear or despair. Instead, they found strength in their unity and camaraderie, supporting each other both emotionally and physically. Their personal stories and experiences, which will forever be etched in the annals of history, serve as a testament to the human spirit's capacity to withstand the most challenging circumstances.

While the hostages endured unimaginable hardships, the Israeli military was working tirelessly behind the scenes to secure their release. Diplomatic efforts and negotiations were conducted in utmost secrecy to ensure the success of the mission. The meticulous planning and coordination by the Israeli intelligence agency, Mossad, played a pivotal role in gathering crucial information and formulating a rescue plan.

The Entebbe rescue mission not only had a profound impact on Israeli society and national identity but also had far-reaching historical and geopolitical implications. It became a symbol of Israeli resilience and determination to protect their citizens, and it highlighted the importance of counterterrorism strategies in the face of growing global threats.

The success of the rescue mission was not solely attributed to the Israeli military's efforts. International support and cooperation played a vital role in its execution. Diplomats from various nations, as well as intelligence agencies worldwide, collaborated to ensure the safe return of the hostages. This united front against terrorism showcased the power of international solidarity in combating such acts of violence.

The media coverage and public perception of the Entebbe hijacking and subsequent rescue were instrumental in shaping global understanding of the event. The stories of the Ugandan hostages, who often remained overlooked, provided a unique perspective on the events at Entebbe and further emphasized the resilience and courage displayed by all those involved.

The aftermath of the Entebbe rescue mission sparked a paradigm shift in counterterrorism strategies worldwide. Governments began to reassess their security measures and prioritize the safety of their citizens. The lessons learned from the mission continue to inform and shape modern counterterrorism efforts.

In conclusion, the acts of resistance and solidarity displayed during the Entebbe rescue mission were nothing short of extraordinary. They serve as a testament to the bravery and resilience of the Israeli people, the importance of international cooperation, and the enduring power of hope in the face of adversity. This chapter aims to shed light on these remarkable acts and pay tribute to the heroes who made the impossible, possible.

The Psychological Toll of Captivity

In the subchapter titled "The Psychological Toll of Captivity," we delve into the profound impact that the harrowing experience of captivity had on the Israeli passengers held hostage during the Entebbe hijacking. This section not only explores the personal stories and experiences of these individuals but also sheds light on the broader psychological implications for both Israeli society and the hostages themselves.

The Israeli passengers endured days of uncertainty, fear, and unimaginable stress while in captivity. Stripped of their freedom and held captive in a foreign land, they faced constant threats to their lives and lived in a state of perpetual anxiety. The subchapter delves into the psychological trauma they endured, examining the long-lasting effects on their mental and emotional well-being.

Through interviews and firsthand accounts, we gain insight into the resilience and strength displayed by the hostages during their captivity. Their stories provide a unique perspective on the human spirit's ability to withstand immense psychological pressure and adapt to extreme circumstances.

Furthermore, this section highlights the critical role of the Israeli military in providing support and comfort to the hostages during their ordeal. The psychological care and rehabilitation efforts implemented by the Israeli military are explored, demonstrating their commitment to the well-being of their citizens and the significant lengths taken to ensure their recovery.

Moreover, the psychological toll experienced by the hostages is contextualized within the broader societal and national identity implications of the Entebbe rescue mission. The subchapter delves into how the mission and its success became a defining moment in Israeli history, fostering national pride, unity, and a renewed sense of purpose.

The psychological trauma faced by the hostages is also examined in the context of counterterrorism strategies. The subchapter delves into how the Israeli government and intelligence agencies, including Mossad, learned from the experience and incorporated psychological support into their future counterterrorism operations.

Lastly, the subchapter sheds light on the aftermath of the rescue mission, exploring the long-term effects on international counterterrorism efforts and the significance of international support and cooperation. It also delves into the media coverage and public perception of the hijacking and subsequent rescue, analyzing how these factors shaped the narrative surrounding the events at Entebbe.

By including the stories and perspectives of the Ugandan hostages, this section offers a comprehensive view of the psychological toll of captivity, encompassing the experiences of both the Israelis and the Ugandans involved. This unique perspective provides a valuable insight into the complex dynamics and psychological impact of the Entebbe hijacking and the subsequent rescue mission.

Liberation and Reintegration

The daring rescue mission at Entebbe, carried out by the Israeli military, stands as a shining testament to the unwavering commitment to protecting its citizens and the lengths to which it will go to ensure their safety. This subchapter will delve into the various aspects surrounding the liberation and reintegration of the hostages, shedding light on the profound impact it had on multiple fronts.

First and foremost, we will explore the personal stories and experiences of the Israeli passengers during their captivity. Through their harrowing tales of fear, resilience, and hope, we gain a deep understanding of the psychological toll exacted by their captors. These accounts not only paint a vivid picture of the hostages' ordeal but also highlight their remarkable spirit and determination to survive.

Behind the scenes, intense diplomatic efforts and negotiations were underway to secure the release of the hostages. This subchapter will delve into the intricate web of political maneuverings, showcasing the delicate balance between the use of force and diplomatic channels. It will provide a captivating account of the tireless efforts made by Israeli diplomats and their allies to bring the mission to a successful conclusion.

The impact of the Entebbe rescue mission on Israeli society and national identity cannot be overstated. This subchapter will explore the profound sense of unity and pride that swept through the nation following the successful operation. It will delve into the ways in which this event served as a rallying cry and a source of inspiration for Israelis, solidifying their resolve to combat terrorism and defend their homeland.

Examining the historical context and geopolitical implications of the hijacking and rescue operation is crucial to understanding the significance of this event. This subchapter will shed light on the broader regional dynamics and the ripple effects that the operation had on global security strategies.

Central to the success of the mission was the role played by the Mossad, the Israeli intelligence agency. Through their meticulous planning and gathering of crucial information, they played a vital role in ensuring the mission's success. This subchapter will delve into the covert operations carried out by the Mossad, highlighting their invaluable contribution.

The aftermath of the Entebbe rescue mission had far-reaching effects on counterterrorism strategies worldwide. This subchapter will explore the long-term implications of the operation, how it reshaped international approaches to combating terrorism, and the lessons learned from this audacious mission.

Lastly, this subchapter will examine the role of international support and cooperation in the success of the rescue mission. It will highlight the invaluable contributions made by allies and partners, showcasing the power of collaboration in the face of adversity.

The media coverage and public perception of the Entebbe hijacking and subsequent rescue will also be explored, shedding light on how this event captivated the world and shaped public opinion.

Finally, we will delve into the stories of the Ugandan hostages, offering a unique perspective on the events at Entebbe from those who were caught in the crossfire. Their experiences and reflections provide a deeply human dimension to this extraordinary event.

Through exploring these multifaceted aspects, this subchapter will provide diplomats and historians with a comprehensive understanding of the Entebbe rescue mission and its wide-ranging impact.

Chapter 3: Diplomatic Efforts and Negotiations behind the Scenes to Secure the Release of the Hostages

The International Response and Support for Israel

The daring rescue mission at Entebbe in 1976 captivated the world's attention and highlighted the immense support for Israel in its time of crisis. Diplomats and historians are well aware of the multifaceted aspects that contributed to the success of the operation, and the subchapter titled "The International Response and Support for Israel" delves into this crucial element of the story.

In this subchapter, we explore the global solidarity that emerged in the face of adversity. Diplomats played a pivotal role in coordinating efforts with various nations to ensure a united front against terrorism. Through diplomatic channels, Israel garnered widespread support, ranging from intelligence sharing to tactical assistance. Historians will find this chapter particularly enlightening, as it provides a comprehensive analysis of the historical context and geopolitical implications of the hijacking and subsequent rescue operation.

Moreover, this subchapter sheds light on the critical role played by the Israeli military and intelligence agency, Mossad. By gathering vital information and meticulously planning the rescue mission, the Israeli military demonstrated their tactical prowess and unwavering commitment to the safety of their citizens. Readers will gain insight into the personal stories and experiences of the Israeli passengers during their captivity, highlighting their resilience and determination to survive.

The diplomatic efforts and negotiations behind the scenes are also explored, revealing the arduous process of securing the release of the hostages. The international support and cooperation that Israel received were instrumental in the success of the rescue mission. This subchapter delves into the strategic alliances formed, the political maneuvering, and the delicate negotiations that took place to bring the hostages home safely.

The impact of the Entebbe rescue mission on Israeli society and national identity is another significant aspect. This subchapter examines how this heroic operation instilled a sense of pride, unity, and resilience within the nation, shaping Israel's future counterterrorism strategies.

The media coverage and public perception of the Entebbe hijacking and subsequent rescue are also analyzed in this subchapter, highlighting the role of the media in shaping the narrative and influencing public opinion.

Lastly, the subchapter delves into the stories of the Ugandan hostages and their unique perspective on the events at Entebbe. By sharing their experiences, readers gain a broader understanding of the human cost and lasting effects of this harrowing ordeal.

Overall, "The International Response and Support for Israel" subchapter provides diplomats and historians with a comprehensive exploration of the multifaceted dynamics that contributed to the success of the Entebbe rescue mission. By understanding the historical, geopolitical, and personal aspects, readers gain a deeper appreciation for the impact of this remarkable event on Israeli society and the international community.

Negotiating with the Hijackers and Ugandan Government

The chapter "Negotiating with the Hijackers and Ugandan Government" delves into the intricate diplomatic efforts and negotiations that took place behind the scenes to secure the release of the hostages during the Entebbe rescue mission. This subchapter provides a comprehensive account of the role played by the Israeli military, highlighting their heroic rescue operation.

The negotiations between the hijackers and the Israeli government were fraught with tension and complexity. Diplomats and historians will gain valuable insights into the challenges faced by the negotiators as they navigated through the demands of the hijackers and the delicate relationship with the Ugandan government.

The chapter also sheds light on the personal stories and experiences of the Israeli passengers during their captivity. By recounting these individual narratives, diplomats and historians will gain a deeper understanding of the emotional and psychological toll endured by the hostages. These personal accounts humanize the events and offer a unique perspective on the resilience and courage displayed by the Israeli passengers.

Furthermore, the subchapter explores the impact of the Entebbe rescue mission on Israeli society and national identity. It analyzes how this daring operation served as a defining moment in Israeli history, uniting the nation and instilling pride in their military capabilities.

The historical context and geopolitical implications of the hijacking and rescue operation are also examined. By providing a comprehensive analysis of the events leading up to the hijacking, diplomats and historians will be able to appreciate the complexity of the situation and the geopolitical ramifications that unfolded as a result.

The role of Mossad, the Israeli intelligence agency, in gathering information and planning the rescue mission is another significant aspect covered in this subchapter. Readers will gain insights into the meticulous planning and intelligence gathering that preceded the operation, showcasing the expertise and effectiveness of Mossad.

Additionally, the aftermath of the Entebbe rescue mission and its long-term effects on counterterrorism strategies are explored. Diplomats and historians will understand how this operation influenced future counterterrorism efforts worldwide and shaped international perceptions of hostage rescue operations.

The subchapter also addresses the role of international support and cooperation in the success of the rescue mission. From the assistance provided by other nations to the collaboration between various intelligence agencies, this chapter highlights the importance of international solidarity in tackling terrorism.

Furthermore, the media coverage and public perception of the Entebbe hijacking and subsequent rescue are examined. Diplomats and historians will gain insights into how the media portrayed these events and how public opinion shaped the narrative surrounding the rescue mission.

Finally, the subchapter delves into the stories of the Ugandan hostages and their perspective on the events at Entebbe. By exploring their experiences and perspectives, readers will gain a more nuanced understanding of the impact of the rescue operation on all those involved.

Overall, this subchapter provides a comprehensive exploration of the negotiations, diplomatic efforts, and personal experiences surrounding the Entebbe rescue mission. It caters to diplomats and historians interested in understanding the multifaceted dimensions of this daring operation and its broader historical and geopolitical implications.

The Role of Diplomatic Channels

One cannot fully comprehend the magnitude of the Entebbe rescue mission without understanding the critical role played by diplomatic channels. As diplomats and historians, it is imperative to delve into the intricate web of negotiations and diplomatic efforts that unfolded behind the scenes, ultimately leading to the successful liberation of the hostages.

When Air France Flight 139 was hijacked by Palestinian terrorists and diverted to Entebbe, Uganda, the Israeli government swiftly initiated diplomatic channels to secure the release of their citizens. These diplomatic efforts involved intense negotiations with Uganda's President Idi Amin, who initially seemed reluctant to cooperate.

The Israeli military's heroic rescue mission was not a standalone operation; it was the result of meticulous planning and intelligence gathering conducted by the Mossad, Israel's intelligence agency. Mossad's vital role in gathering information about the hijackers, their demands, and the layout of the airport proved invaluable in formulating a successful rescue plan. Their intelligence was shared with diplomatic channels, enabling negotiators to navigate the intricacies of the situation.

International support and cooperation were crucial to the success of the rescue mission. Diplomatic pressure exerted by various countries, including the United States and France, played a pivotal role in securing the release of the hostages. Diplomats worked tirelessly behind closed doors, leveraging their relationships and influence to rally support for Israel's cause.

The aftermath of the Entebbe rescue mission had a profound impact on Israeli society and national identity. The audaciousness and success of the mission solidified Israel's reputation as a formidable military power and boosted national morale. The rescue mission became a source of inspiration and pride for Israelis, symbolizing their unwavering commitment to the safety and well-being of their citizens.

The media coverage and public perception of the Entebbe hijacking and subsequent rescue cannot be overlooked. Journalists from around the world flocked to Uganda to capture the unfolding events, bringing the plight of the hostages to the forefront of global attention. This extensive media coverage contributed to public support for the rescue mission and heightened international pressure on the hijackers.

While much attention has been given to the Israeli passengers and their experiences during captivity, it is also crucial to examine the stories and perspectives of the Ugandan hostages. Their voices provide a unique insight into the events at Entebbe, shedding light on the complex dynamics between captives and captors and the impact of the rescue mission on their lives.

In conclusion, the role of diplomatic channels in the Entebbe rescue mission cannot be overstated. These channels were instrumental in gathering intelligence, negotiating with the hijackers and Ugandan authorities, rallying international support, and ultimately ensuring the success of the mission. By exploring this crucial aspect of the Entebbe operation, diplomats and historians gain a more comprehensive understanding of the historical context, geopolitical implications, and long-term effects of this remarkable rescue mission.

Challenges and Breakthroughs in the Negotiations

The Entebbe rescue mission stands as a testament to the unwavering determination and courage of the Israeli military. However, behind this heroic operation, a series of challenges and breakthroughs in the negotiations took place, shaping the outcome of this historic event. This subchapter delves into the intricate web of diplomatic efforts and the behind-the-scenes negotiations that eventually led to the successful release of the hostages.

One of the major challenges faced during the negotiations was the complexity of the geopolitical landscape. The hijacking of Air France Flight 139 by Palestinian and German terrorists took place in the heart of Africa, under the regime of Ugandan dictator Idi Amin. This necessitated delicate diplomacy with multiple actors, including the Ugandan government, the terrorists, and other international entities involved.

The role of the Israeli military in the rescue mission at Entebbe added another layer of complexity. As negotiations progressed, the Israeli military had to balance the delicate task of maintaining the safety of the hostages while simultaneously preparing for a potential military intervention. This dynamic required careful coordination and precise decision-making to ensure the success of the operation.

One of the most significant breakthroughs in the negotiations came through the covert efforts of Mossad, the Israeli intelligence agency. Their meticulous gathering of information and strategic planning played a crucial role in providing a sound basis for negotiations. The intelligence gathered by Mossad not only helped to identify the terrorists and their demands but also provided critical insights into the Ugandan government's involvement.

The negotiations reached a pivotal moment when Israel managed to secure international support and cooperation. Diplomats from various countries, including France, Germany, and the United States, rallied behind Israel's cause. This support not only added weight to the negotiations but also helped to isolate the terrorists and exert pressure on the Ugandan government.

The breakthrough finally came when Israel's negotiations team, led by then-Defense Minister Shimon Peres, successfully convinced the terrorists to agree to release the non-Israeli hostages. This crucial breakthrough laid the foundation for the subsequent military operation and the eventual release of all the hostages.

The challenges faced, and the breakthroughs achieved during the negotiations surrounding the Entebbe rescue mission, had far-reaching implications. Not only did this operation solidify the role of the Israeli military in counterterrorism efforts, but it also galvanized Israeli society and reinforced national identity. Furthermore, the success of the mission paved the way for the development of new counterterrorism strategies globally.

In conclusion, the challenges and breakthroughs in the negotiations surrounding the Entebbe rescue mission were instrumental in shaping its outcome. The delicate diplomacy, intelligence gathering, and international cooperation were all crucial elements in ensuring the success of the operation. This chapter sheds light on the intricacies of the negotiations, highlighting the immense efforts undertaken to secure the release of the hostages and the geopolitical implications that followed.

The Final Agreement and Release of the Hostages

In this subchapter titled "The Final Agreement and Release of the Hostages," we delve into the climactic conclusion of the Entebbe rescue mission, a historic event that captivated the world and forever changed the landscape of counterterrorism operations. Addressing an audience of diplomats and historians, we explore the multifaceted aspects that contributed to the mission's success and its profound impact on Israeli society and national identity.

The Israeli military's role in the rescue mission at Entebbe stands as a testament to their unwavering commitment and daring courage. We delve into the intricacies of the operation, highlighting the meticulous planning, the audacious execution, and the sheer bravery of the soldiers involved. Their personal stories and experiences during their captivity are shared, offering a poignant glimpse into the adversity they faced and the resilience they displayed.

Behind the scenes, diplomatic efforts and negotiations played a pivotal role in securing the release of the hostages. We shed light on the intricate maneuvering and delicate negotiations that took place, showcasing the diplomatic finesse required to navigate through this high-stakes situation.

Examining the historical context and geopolitical implications of the hijacking and rescue operation, we unveil the intricate web of events that led to this critical juncture. The role of Mossad, the Israeli intelligence agency, in gathering information and planning the rescue mission is explored, shedding light on the intelligence prowess that underpinned this audacious operation.

The aftermath of the Entebbe rescue mission and its long-term effects on counterterrorism strategies receive due attention. We analyze how this operation reshaped global approaches to combating terrorism and influenced the development of sophisticated strategies and tactics.

International support and cooperation played a pivotal role in the success of the rescue mission. We delve into the various nations and organizations that rallied behind Israel, demonstrating the power of collaboration in the face of adversity.

The media coverage and public perception of the Entebbe hijacking and subsequent rescue are examined, revealing the significant role played by the media in shaping public opinion and capturing the world's attention.

Lastly, we explore the stories and perspectives of the Ugandan hostages, giving voice to their experiences and shedding light on their unique perspective on the events at Entebbe.

In "The Final Agreement and Release of the Hostages," we unravel the captivating climax of the Entebbe rescue mission, providing a comprehensive exploration of its historical, geopolitical, and human dimensions.

Chapter 4: The Impact of the Entebbe Rescue Mission on Israeli Society and National Identity

The Symbolic Importance of Entebbe in Israeli History

The Entebbe rescue mission, also known as Operation Thunderbolt, holds a significant place in Israeli history. This subchapter explores the symbolic importance of the mission and its enduring impact on Israeli society and national identity. Addressed to diplomats and historians, it provides a comprehensive analysis of the historical context, geopolitical implications, and personal stories surrounding this remarkable event.

The Entebbe rescue mission showcased the unwavering resolve and bravery of the Israeli military. It demonstrated Israel's commitment to protecting its citizens, even in the face of unimaginable odds. This chapter delves into the role of the Israeli military in planning and executing the daring rescue operation, highlighting the meticulous planning and impeccable execution that unfolded on that fateful day.

The personal stories and experiences of the Israeli passengers during their captivity form an integral part of this narrative. By recounting their harrowing ordeals, this subchapter aims to shed light on the unimaginable strength and resilience displayed by these individuals. Their stories provide a human perspective and offer a deeper understanding of the psychological impact of the hijacking and subsequent rescue.

Behind the scenes, diplomatic efforts and negotiations were crucial in securing the release of the hostages. This chapter explores the delicate diplomatic maneuvers and the role of international support and cooperation in the success of the mission. It highlights the complexities involved in navigating political landscapes and underscores the significance of global solidarity in the face of terrorism.

The media coverage and public perception of the Entebbe hijacking and rescue mission are also examined. This subchapter delves into the way these events were portrayed in the media and how they shaped public opinion both within Israel and abroad. It analyzes the lasting impact of this media coverage on counterterrorism strategies and the broader fight against terrorism.

Furthermore, the subchapter delves into the historical context and geopolitical implications of the hijacking and rescue operation. It explores the implications for Israeli-Ugandan relations, as well as the wider regional dynamics in the Middle East during that period. The role of Mossad, the Israeli intelligence agency, in gathering crucial information and planning the rescue mission is also explored, shedding light on the intricate web of intelligence operations.

Lastly, this subchapter examines the aftermath of the Entebbe rescue mission and its long-term effects on counterterrorism strategies. It analyzes how this operation influenced subsequent approaches to hostage situations and counterterrorism efforts worldwide.

In conclusion, the symbolic importance of Entebbe in Israeli history cannot be overstated. This subchapter delves into the multifaceted dimensions of this event, catering to the interests of diplomats and historians alike. By examining the role of the Israeli military, personal stories of the hostages, diplomatic efforts, and geopolitical implications, it offers a comprehensive understanding of the lasting impact of the Entebbe rescue mission on Israeli society, national identity, and the fight against terrorism.

Strengthening of National Unity and Pride

The Entebbe rescue mission was not only a remarkable military operation but also a defining moment in Israeli history that profoundly impacted national unity and pride. The audacity and success of the mission served as a powerful symbol of Israel's resolve to protect its citizens and project its military capabilities on a global stage. This subchapter aims to explore the multifaceted dimensions of how the Entebbe operation strengthened the Israeli society and national identity.

Firstly, the rescue mission showcased the unparalleled bravery and professionalism of the Israeli military. Diplomats and historians will delve into the meticulous planning, strategizing, and execution of the operation, highlighting the ingenuity and resourcefulness of the Israeli Defense Forces (IDF). By recounting the heroic actions of the soldiers involved, this chapter will underline the unwavering commitment of the IDF to safeguard Israeli lives, fostering a sense of national pride and admiration for the military's capabilities.

Moreover, the personal stories and experiences of the Israeli passengers held captive at Entebbe Airport will be shared to provide a firsthand account of their ordeal. Understanding their resilience and courage during their captivity will further deepen the audience's appreciation for their unwavering spirit and determination. The survivors' narratives will not only highlight their individual acts of bravery but also showcase the collective unity and support that emerged among the captives, reinforcing the strength of the Israeli people in the face of adversity.

The diplomatic efforts and negotiations behind the scenes to secure the release of the hostages will also be explored. This will shed light on the importance of international cooperation and support in the success of the rescue mission. The subchapter will highlight the tireless efforts of Israeli diplomats who worked tirelessly to rally international support and navigate the complex political landscape to secure the freedom of their compatriots.

Furthermore, the impact of the Entebbe rescue mission on Israeli society cannot be underestimated. The audacious operation not only bolstered national pride but also united the nation like never before. Israelis from all walks of life were unified in their support for the military and their belief in the country's resilience. This chapter will delve into the long-term effects of the operation, including its influence on counterterrorism strategies and the strengthening of Israel's position in the world.

In conclusion, the Entebbe rescue mission was a pivotal moment in Israeli history that solidified national unity and pride. By exploring the role of the Israeli military, the personal stories of the hostages, the diplomatic efforts, and the impact on society, this subchapter aims to provide a comprehensive understanding of the profound effects of the operation on Israel's national identity and the pride of its people.

The Impact on Israeli Politics and Leadership

The Entebbe rescue mission had a profound impact on Israeli politics and leadership, shaping the course of the nation's history and its approach to counterterrorism. The daring operation not only showcased the Israeli military's capabilities but also had far-reaching implications for Israeli society, national identity, and international relations.

At the time of the hijacking, Israel was still reeling from the trauma of the Munich Olympics massacre in 1972. The successful rescue mission at Entebbe served as a turning point, restoring faith in the Israeli military and bolstering national pride. Prime Minister Yitzhak Rabin's decisive leadership and the courage displayed by the Israeli commandos further solidified their positions as national heroes.

The Entebbe mission also had a significant impact on Israeli politics. Rabin's handling of the crisis garnered widespread support and boosted his political standing, ultimately leading to his election as Prime Minister in 1974. The success of the operation propelled Rabin's reputation as a strong leader and contributed to the political stability of Israel during a turbulent period.

Furthermore, the Entebbe rescue mission highlighted the crucial role of intelligence agencies like Mossad in gathering information and planning such operations. Mossad's meticulous planning and execution of the rescue demonstrated the agency's capabilities and earned it international recognition as one of the world's most effective intelligence agencies.

Internationally, the Entebbe rescue mission showcased Israel's determination to protect its citizens and fight against terrorism. The operation received widespread support and admiration from countries around the world, strengthening Israel's diplomatic standing in the global arena.

The media coverage and public perception of the Entebbe hijacking and subsequent rescue were also instrumental in shaping Israeli politics and leadership. The images of Israeli commandos freeing the hostages resonated with people worldwide, further solidifying Israel's image as a resilient and determined nation.

The long-term effects of the Entebbe rescue mission on counterterrorism strategies cannot be overstated. The success of the operation served as a model for future hostage rescue missions and prompted other countries to reassess their own counterterrorism tactics.

In conclusion, the impact of the Entebbe rescue mission on Israeli politics and leadership was profound. It not only restored faith in the

Israeli military and bolstered national pride but also showcased the importance of intelligence agencies like Mossad. The operation had far-reaching implications for Israeli society, national identity, and international relations, shaping Israel's approach to counterterrorism and solidifying its position as a determined and resilient nation.

Lessons Learned and Changes in Counterterrorism Strategies

The Entebbe rescue mission was a defining moment in the history of counterterrorism, and its impact on Israeli society and national identity cannot be overstated. This subchapter will delve into the numerous lessons learned from this harrowing event and the subsequent changes in counterterrorism strategies that emerged as a result.

One of the key takeaways from the Entebbe rescue mission was the importance of intelligence gathering and planning. The role of Mossad, the Israeli intelligence agency, in gathering crucial information about the hijackers and the layout of the airport was instrumental in the success of the operation. This led to a greater emphasis on intelligence sharing and cooperation between international intelligence agencies, recognizing that a global approach is needed to combat the threat of terrorism effectively.

The aftermath of the Entebbe rescue mission also prompted a reevaluation of hostage negotiation tactics. While diplomatic efforts were made behind the scenes to secure the release of the hostages, it became evident that negotiations alone were not always sufficient. The use of force, when necessary and well-coordinated, was deemed a viable option to ensure the safety of innocent lives. This shift in mindset influenced future counterterrorism operations and highlighted the need for specialized units capable of executing complex and high-risk missions.

Furthermore, the Entebbe rescue mission brought international support and cooperation to the forefront. The success of the operation was due in part to the collaboration between Israel and other nations, including Kenya, whose assistance in providing a refueling stop for the Israeli planes was pivotal. This highlighted the importance of building alliances and fostering international cooperation to combat terrorism effectively.

In terms of media coverage and public perception, the Entebbe rescue mission captured the imagination of people worldwide. The daring nature of the operation and the successful rescue of hostages created a sense of national pride in Israel, but it also brought attention to the global threat of terrorism. This increased awareness led to public support for tougher counterterrorism measures and a greater understanding of the challenges faced by nations in the fight against terrorism.

Finally, the subchapter will explore the stories and perspectives of the Ugandan hostages. Their experiences shed light on the trauma endured during their captivity and provide a unique insight into the events at Entebbe from their perspective. Understanding their stories is crucial for a comprehensive understanding of the impact of the rescue mission.

In conclusion, the Entebbe rescue mission served as a catalyst for significant changes in counterterrorism strategies. From intelligence gathering to hostage negotiation tactics, international cooperation to public perception, this subchapter will analyze the lessons learned from this historic event and the lasting effects it had on counterterrorism efforts worldwide.

The Lasting Legacy of Entebbe in Israeli Culture

The Entebbe rescue mission of 1976 stands as a pivotal moment in Israeli history, forever etched into the nation's collective memory. This subchapter explores the profound and lasting impact of the operation on Israeli culture, illuminating its significance to diplomats and historians alike.

The role of the Israeli military in the rescue mission at Entebbe showcased their unwavering commitment to protecting their citizens, even in the face of seemingly insurmountable odds. This extraordinary display of bravery and skill elevated the Israeli military's reputation to unprecedented heights, solidifying their position as a force to be reckoned with.

The personal stories and experiences of the Israeli passengers during their captivity provide a deeply human perspective on the events at Entebbe. Their resilience and courage in the face of adversity serve as a testament to the indomitable spirit of the Israeli people.

Behind the scenes, diplomatic efforts and negotiations were instrumental in securing the release of the hostages. This subchapter delves into the intricate web of diplomatic maneuvering and the tireless efforts of Israeli officials to navigate the complex geopolitical landscape of the time.

The Entebbe rescue mission had a profound impact on Israeli society and national identity. It united the nation, fostering a sense of national pride and solidarity that continues to resonate today. The courage and determination displayed by the rescue team and the rescued hostages became symbols of Israeli resilience and the unwavering commitment to protect its citizens.

The historical context and geopolitical implications of the hijacking and rescue operation are explored in this subchapter. It analyzes the intricate web of international relations and the delicate balancing act Israel had to maintain to execute the mission successfully.

The crucial role of Mossad, the Israeli intelligence agency, is examined in this subchapter. It delves into their meticulous gathering of information and strategic planning, highlighting their invaluable contribution to the success of the rescue mission.

The aftermath of the Entebbe rescue mission had far-reaching effects on counterterrorism strategies worldwide. It influenced the way nations approached hijackings and terrorist threats, serving as a model for future operations.

International support and cooperation played a pivotal role in the success of the rescue mission. This subchapter examines the alliances forged and the assistance provided by various nations, underscoring the significance of international solidarity in times of crisis.

The media coverage and public perception of the Entebbe hijacking and subsequent rescue are also explored. It delves into the ways in which the media portrayed the events, shaping public opinion and leaving an indelible mark on the collective consciousness.

Finally, this subchapter sheds light on the stories of the Ugandan hostages, providing a perspective often overlooked. It examines their experiences and perspectives on the events at Entebbe, offering a comprehensive understanding of the multifaceted nature of this historic event.

In conclusion, the lasting legacy of Entebbe in Israeli culture is profound and far-reaching. This subchapter offers a comprehensive examination of the historical, geopolitical, and cultural implications of the rescue mission, providing diplomats and historians with a deeper understanding of this pivotal moment in Israeli history.

Chapter 5: The Historical Context and Geopolitical Implications of the Hijacking and Rescue Operation

The Rise of International Terrorism in the 1970s

In the tumultuous 1970s, international terrorism reached a new level of prominence, and one of the most iconic incidents during this era was the hijacking of Air France Flight 139 to Entebbe Airport in Uganda. This subchapter will explore the historical context, geopolitical implications, and the various elements that contributed to the rise of international terrorism during this period.

The hijacking of Flight 139 on June 27, 1976, by members of the Popular Front for the Liberation of Palestine (PFLP) and the German Revolutionary Cells shocked the world. The incident highlighted the vulnerability of civil aviation and marked a turning point in terrorist tactics. It was no longer confined to local conflicts but became a global phenomenon.

The Israeli military's heroic rescue mission at Entebbe showcased their unparalleled skill and determination. This subchapter will delve into the role of the Israeli military in planning and executing the daring operation, highlighting the bravery and resourcefulness of the soldiers involved.

Furthermore, the personal stories and experiences of the Israeli passengers during their captivity will provide a unique perspective on the ordeal they endured. Their accounts will shed light on the psychological and physical hardships they faced and the resilience they displayed in the face of adversity.

Behind the scenes, diplomatic efforts and negotiations were underway to secure the release of the hostages. This subchapter will examine the delicate diplomatic dance that took place, exploring the intricate strategies employed by Israeli diplomats and their international counterparts.

The impact of the Entebbe rescue mission on Israeli society and national identity cannot be overstated. This subchapter will explore how the successful operation boosted national morale, instilled a sense of pride, and bolstered Israel's image on the global stage.

The role of Mossad, the Israeli intelligence agency, in gathering vital information and meticulously planning the rescue mission will be examined. Their crucial contributions and their incredible ability to infiltrate and extract intelligence will be highlighted.

The aftermath of the Entebbe rescue mission had far-reaching effects on counterterrorism strategies worldwide. This subchapter will delve into the long-term implications, analyzing how governments and security agencies around the world adapted their tactics and strategies in response to this watershed moment.

Additionally, the role of international support and cooperation in the success of the rescue mission will be explored. The subchapter will discuss the nations and organizations that rallied behind Israel, showcasing the power of international collaboration in combating terrorism.

The media coverage and public perception of the Entebbe hijacking and subsequent rescue will also be analyzed. This subchapter will delve into how the events were portrayed in the media and how public opinion shifted as the situation unfolded.

Finally, the subchapter will shed light on the stories of the Ugandan hostages and their perspective on the events at Entebbe. It will provide a unique glimpse into the experiences and emotions of those who were caught in the crossfire, emphasizing the impact of the incident on their lives.

In conclusion, the rise of international terrorism in the 1970s, exemplified by the Entebbe hijacking and rescue mission, not only marked a turning point in global security but also had profound implications for Israeli society, counterterrorism strategies, and the geopolitical landscape. Understanding the historical context and multifaceted aspects of this event is crucial for diplomats and historians alike.

The Political Climate in the Middle East at the Time

In order to fully understand the significance of the Israeli military's heroic rescue mission at Entebbe, it is crucial to delve into the political climate that prevailed in the Middle East during that time. This subchapter aims to provide diplomats and historians with a comprehensive analysis of the regional dynamics that influenced the events leading up to the Entebbe hijacking and subsequent rescue operation.

During the 1970s, the Middle East was grappling with a multitude of challenges, including the Israeli-Arab conflict, the rise of Palestinian militant groups, and the repercussions of the Yom Kippur War. The Entebbe hijacking occurred in the midst of this tense atmosphere, adding another layer of complexity to an already volatile region.

The political landscape in the Arab world was particularly crucial in understanding the motivations behind the hijacking. The hijackers, members of the Popular Front for the Liberation of Palestine (PFLP), sought to gain attention for their cause and exert pressure on Israel through their actions. This incident highlighted the growing influence of radical Palestinian factions and their impact on regional stability.

Simultaneously, the Israeli government was facing immense pressure to safeguard its citizens and maintain national security. The Entebbe rescue mission was a testament to Israel's determination to protect its people, even in the face of seemingly insurmountable odds. It showcased the Israeli military's capability and willingness to go to great lengths to ensure the safety of its citizens, further solidifying national identity and pride.

Behind the scenes, diplomatic efforts and negotiations were underway to secure the release of the hostages. The involvement of various international actors, including the United States and Kenya, played a crucial role in the eventual success of the rescue operation. The collaboration between these nations showcased the importance of international support and cooperation in combating terrorism and ensuring global security.

Furthermore, the Entebbe rescue mission had far-reaching implications for counterterrorism strategies. It demonstrated the necessity of proactive measures and intelligence gathering in preventing future hijackings. The role of Mossad, the Israeli intelligence agency, in gathering information and planning the rescue mission was paramount to its success.

In the aftermath of the Entebbe rescue mission, media coverage and public perception played a significant role in shaping the narrative surrounding the events. The heroic actions of the Israeli military garnered international attention and admiration, further highlighting the importance of media in shaping public opinion and influencing political outcomes.

Lastly, exploring the stories and perspectives of the Ugandan hostages provides a unique insight into their experiences at Entebbe. Their voices and testimonies shed light on the impact of the hijacking on their lives and the long-lasting trauma they endured.

By examining the political climate in the Middle East at the time, diplomats and historians can gain a deeper understanding of the historical context and geopolitical implications of the Entebbe hijacking and subsequent rescue operation. The subchapter aims to provide a comprehensive analysis of the regional dynamics, diplomatic efforts, and long-term effects of this significant event.

The Impact on Israeli-Ugandan Relations

The Entebbe rescue mission in 1976 was a pivotal moment in Israeli-Ugandan relations, leaving a lasting impact on both countries. This subchapter will delve into the historical context and geopolitical implications of the hijacking and subsequent rescue operation, shedding light on the diplomatic efforts, personal stories, and long-term effects of this extraordinary event.

The hijacking of an Air France plane and the subsequent hostage crisis at Entebbe Airport in Uganda presented a unique challenge for Israel. With Israeli citizens among the hostages, the Israeli military swiftly mobilized to plan a daring rescue mission. This chapter will explore the role of the Israeli military in executing this operation and the personal stories and experiences of the Israeli passengers during their captivity.

Behind the scenes, diplomatic efforts and negotiations were underway to secure the release of the hostages. Diplomats worked tirelessly to navigate the delicate political landscape, seeking international support and cooperation. This subchapter will unveil the diplomatic intricacies and shed light on the role of Mossad, the Israeli intelligence agency, in gathering crucial information and planning the rescue mission.

The Entebbe rescue mission had profound implications for Israeli society and national identity. It became a symbol of Israeli bravery and determination, boosting morale and reinforcing a sense of national unity. This chapter will delve into the impact on Israeli society and explore how the events at Entebbe shaped Israel's counterterrorism strategies in the long run.

Furthermore, this subchapter will highlight the stories of the Ugandan hostages and their perspective on the events at Entebbe. Their firsthand accounts will provide a unique viewpoint and shed light on the complex dynamics and emotions surrounding the hijacking and rescue operation.

The international media coverage and public perception of the Entebbe hijacking and subsequent rescue were also significant. This chapter will examine the media's role in shaping public opinion and explore how the world reacted to this audacious rescue mission.

Lastly, the aftermath of the Entebbe rescue mission will be analyzed, focusing on its long-term effects on counterterrorism strategies globally. By examining the impact on Israeli-Ugandan relations, this chapter will provide valuable insights for diplomats and historians, shedding light on a remarkable event that continues to reverberate through history.

Geopolitical Implications for Africa and the World

The Entebbe rescue mission, undoubtedly one of the most daring and heroic military operations in history, had far-reaching geopolitical implications for Africa and the world. This subchapter explores the broader context, diplomatic efforts, and aftermath of the events at Entebbe, shedding light on the profound impact it had on various aspects of international relations.

At the heart of the mission was the Israeli military's role in executing the rescue operation. Their unparalleled bravery and strategic planning showcased Israel's military capabilities, raising their global profile and establishing them as a force to be reckoned with. This chapter delves into the intricacies of the mission, highlighting the personal stories and experiences of the Israeli passengers during their harrowing captivity.

Behind the scenes, intense diplomatic efforts and negotiations were underway to secure the release of the hostages. This subchapter dives into the delicate balance of diplomatic maneuvering, exploring the roles played by various countries, international organizations, and individuals in ensuring the success of the rescue mission.

The Entebbe rescue mission became a pivotal moment in Israeli society and its national identity. This chapter examines the profound impact it had on the nation, including the strengthening of their resolve in the face of terrorism and the reevaluation of their counterterrorism strategies.

To fully understand the geopolitical implications of the hijacking and rescue operation, the historical context is essential. This subchapter delves into the broader political dynamics of the time, analyzing how the events at Entebbe reverberated across Africa and the world.

A crucial element in the success of the rescue mission was the role of Mossad, the Israeli intelligence agency. This chapter uncovers the intricate web of information gathering and planning that preceded the operation, highlighting Mossad's crucial contributions.

The aftermath of the Entebbe rescue mission had significant long-term effects on counterterrorism strategies worldwide. This subchapter explores the ripple effects, including changes in international security protocols, the emergence of new strategies, and the impact on future hostage rescue operations.

International support and cooperation were paramount to the success of the rescue mission. This subchapter delves into the role played by various countries and organizations in providing assistance and facilitating the operation.

The media coverage and public perception of the Entebbe hijacking and subsequent rescue also played a significant role. This chapter explores how the media shaped public opinion and the lasting impact it had on the global understanding of terrorism.

Finally, this subchapter sheds light on the stories and perspectives of the Ugandan hostages, offering a unique insight into the events at Entebbe from their point of view.

In conclusion, the geopolitical implications of the Entebbe rescue mission were far-reaching. This subchapter provides a comprehensive analysis of the mission's impact on Israeli society, international relations, counterterrorism strategies, and the broader historical context of the time. Diplomats and historians alike will find this exploration of the Entebbe rescue mission to be a compelling and illuminating read.

Lessons for International Security and Counterterrorism Efforts

Title: Lessons for International Security and Counterterrorism Efforts

Introduction:

The subchapter "Lessons for International Security and Counterterrorism Efforts" within the book "Entebbe Unveiled: The Israeli Military's Heroic Rescue Mission" offers valuable insights for diplomats and historians. This section delves into various aspects surrounding the Entebbe rescue mission, shedding light on its impact on Israeli society, the diplomatic efforts involved, and the historical context and geopolitical implications of the hijacking and rescue. It also explores the personal stories of Israeli passengers, the role of Mossad, international support, and the media coverage surrounding this extraordinary event.

1. The Role of the Israeli Military in the Rescue Mission at Entebbe:

This section highlights the exceptional bravery and strategic planning exhibited by the Israeli military during the rescue operation. It analyzes their tactical approach, highlighting the lessons that can be learned for future counterterrorism efforts.

2. The Personal Stories and Experiences of the Israeli Passengers During Their Captivity:

By sharing firsthand accounts from the Israeli hostages, this section offers a unique perspective on the emotional and psychological toll endured during their captivity. Diplomats and historians can gain a deeper understanding of the human aspect of such crises.

3. Diplomatic Efforts and Negotiations Behind the Scenes to Secure the Release of the Hostages:

Exploring the diplomatic negotiations that took place behind closed doors, this segment examines the intricate negotiations and diplomatic maneuvering that ultimately led to the successful rescue mission.

4. The Impact of the Entebbe Rescue Mission on Israeli Society and National Identity:

This part focuses on the transformational effect the Entebbe rescue had on Israeli society. It explores how the mission bolstered national pride and solidified Israel's commitment to protecting its citizens, shaping the nation's identity for years to come.

5. The Historical Context and Geopolitical Implications of the Hijacking and Rescue Operation:

Providing historical context, this section delves into the geopolitical implications of the Entebbe hijacking. It explores the global response and the ramifications for international relations and counterterrorism strategies.

6. The Role of Mossad in Gathering Information and Planning the Rescue Mission:

This segment delves into the intelligence-gathering efforts of Mossad, Israel's renowned intelligence agency. It reveals the meticulous planning and intelligence operations that culminated in the successful rescue mission.

7. The Aftermath of the Entebbe Rescue Mission and Its Long-Term Effects on Counterterrorism Strategies:

Examining the long-term effects of the Entebbe rescue mission, this section explores how the operation shaped subsequent counterterrorism strategies worldwide. It analyzes the lessons learned and their impact on international security efforts.

8. The Role of International Support and Cooperation in the Success of the Rescue Mission:

Highlighting the significance of international support, this segment examines the collaborative efforts that contributed to the successful outcome of the Entebbe rescue mission. It underscores the importance of cooperation in combating terrorism.

9. The Media Coverage and Public Perception of the Entebbe Hijacking and Subsequent Rescue:

This part delves into the media coverage and public perception of the Entebbe hijacking and subsequent rescue mission. It explores how the media played a role in shaping public opinion and understanding of the event.

10. The Stories of the Ugandan Hostages and Their Perspective on the Events at Entebbe:

Offering a different perspective, this section shares the experiences and stories of the Ugandan hostages. It sheds light on their ordeal and provides a deeper understanding of the events from their point of view.

Conclusion:

The subchapter "Lessons for International Security and Counterterrorism Efforts" provides diplomats and historians with a comprehensive analysis of the Entebbe rescue mission. By examining various aspects such as the role of the Israeli military, diplomatic efforts, intelligence operations, and the impact on Israeli society, readers will gain valuable insights into the significance of this historic event in the context of international security and counterterrorism.

Chapter 6: The Role of Mossad (Israeli Intelligence Agency) in Gathering Information and Planning the Rescue Mission

Mossad's Intelligence Gathering and Analysis

The success of the daring Entebbe rescue mission was due in large part to the exceptional intelligence gathering and analysis carried out by the Mossad, Israel's renowned intelligence agency. This subchapter explores the pivotal role played by Mossad in gathering information and planning the mission, shedding light on their strategic brilliance and meticulous attention to detail.

Mossad's intelligence gathering efforts began immediately after the hijacking of Air France Flight 139 by Palestinian and German terrorists. With the lives of over 100 Israeli hostages at stake, Mossad spared no effort in collecting crucial information to aid in the planning of the rescue operation. Through a vast network of informants, agents, and cutting-edge surveillance technology, Mossad meticulously monitored the movements and intentions of the hijackers, as well as the Ugandan government's response to the crisis.

The agency's analysts sifted through mountains of data, deciphering intercepted communications, and piecing together the puzzle that would ultimately lead to the successful execution of the rescue mission. By meticulously studying the layout of Entebbe Airport and obtaining blueprints of the terminal building, Mossad was able to plan every intricate detail of the operation, including the precise timing, routes, and contingencies.

Moreover, Mossad's intelligence gathering went beyond the immediate crisis at hand. The agency delved into the historical context and geopolitical implications of the hijacking, uncovering the hidden motivations and alliances behind the terrorist act. This subchapter delves into the historical context, shedding light on the complex web of regional tensions and power dynamics that gave rise to the hijacking and subsequent rescue mission.

Furthermore, the aftermath of the Entebbe rescue mission had far-reaching implications for counterterrorism strategies globally. The subchapter explores the long-term effects of the operation on Israel's national identity and society, as well as its influence on international counterterrorism efforts. It also delves into the impact of the mission on future hostage rescue operations, shaping the strategies employed by other nations in similar crises.

Through interviews with key Mossad operatives, diplomats, and historians, this subchapter provides a comprehensive account of Mossad's intelligence gathering and analysis during the Entebbe rescue mission. It offers a unique insight into the agency's invaluable contributions to the operation's success and its enduring impact on Israeli society, national identity, and global counterterrorism strategies.

Infiltrating the Hijackers' Network

In this subchapter of "Entebbe Unveiled: The Israeli Military's Heroic Rescue Mission," we delve into the intricate web of the hijackers' network that held the Israeli passengers captive at Entebbe Airport. Addressed to diplomats and historians, we aim to provide a comprehensive understanding of the events surrounding the rescue mission while satisfying the interests of our niche audience.

The Israeli military played a central role in the Entebbe rescue mission, and this subchapter sheds light on their strategic approach. We explore how they infiltrated the hijackers' network, gathering vital intelligence from Mossad, the Israeli intelligence agency. Through meticulous planning and execution, the military devised a daring operation to free the hostages, showcasing their exceptional skills and resourcefulness.

While the military's efforts were commendable, we also delve into the personal stories and experiences of the Israeli passengers during their captivity. Their resilience and determination in the face of adversity provide a compelling narrative that humanizes the events at Entebbe. By highlighting their stories, we shed light on the emotional toll and the strength of the human spirit amidst unimaginable circumstances.

Behind the scenes, diplomatic efforts and negotiations were underway to secure the release of the hostages. We delve into the intricate diplomatic maneuvers that took place, showcasing the delicate balance between political considerations and the urgency of saving lives. These negotiations had far-reaching implications, not only for the hostages but also for the geopolitical landscape at the time.

The impact of the Entebbe rescue mission on Israeli society and national identity cannot be overstated. We explore how this extraordinary event galvanized the nation, strengthening their resolve against terrorism and providing a beacon of hope in a tumultuous time. The long-term effects on counterterrorism strategies are also examined, as the Entebbe mission served as a blueprint for future operations.

International support and cooperation played a crucial role in the success of the rescue mission. We highlight the collaborative efforts between Israel and other nations, underscoring the significance of global solidarity in combating terrorism. Additionally, we analyze the media coverage and public perception of the Entebbe hijacking and subsequent rescue, shedding light on how these events were portrayed and perceived around the world.

Finally, we provide a unique perspective by delving into the stories of the Ugandan hostages. Their experiences and viewpoints offer a comprehensive understanding of the events at Entebbe from a different lens, allowing for a more nuanced analysis of the overall situation.

"Infiltrating the Hijackers' Network" encapsulates the multifaceted aspects of the Entebbe rescue mission, catering to the interests of diplomats and historians alike. By examining the military's role, personal narratives, diplomatic efforts, and historical context, we provide a comprehensive and engaging account of this pivotal moment in history.

Coordinating with the Israeli Military

In the face of one of the most audacious acts of terrorism in history, the Israeli military played a pivotal role in the heroic rescue mission at Entebbe. Their unwavering determination and meticulous planning were crucial in the successful execution of this daring operation. This subchapter explores the coordination efforts undertaken by the Israeli military and the extraordinary individuals involved.

From the moment news broke of the hijacking of Air France Flight 139, the Israeli military swiftly mobilized its forces. Under the command of General Yitzhak Rabin, a team of elite soldiers from the Israeli Defense Forces (IDF) was assembled to carry out the rescue mission. This chapter delves into the role of the Israeli military in the mission, examining their strategies, tactics, and the challenges they faced.

While the Israeli passengers endured unimaginable hardships during their captivity, their strength and resilience were truly inspiring. Through personal accounts and interviews, readers gain an intimate understanding of the experiences of these individuals, their fears, hopes, and the courage that sustained them throughout their ordeal.

Behind the scenes, diplomatic efforts and negotiations were in full swing to secure the release of the hostages. This subchapter delves into the intricate web of political maneuvering and delicate negotiations that took place, shedding light on the pivotal role played by diplomats in resolving this crisis.

The impact of the Entebbe rescue mission on Israeli society and national identity cannot be overstated. This chapter explores the profound effect this event had on the collective psyche of the nation, fueling a sense of unity, national pride, and determination to combat terrorism. The historical context and geopolitical implications of the hijacking and rescue operation are also examined, providing readers with a comprehensive understanding of this significant moment in history.

Integral to the success of the rescue mission was the role of Mossad, the Israeli intelligence agency. This subchapter delves into the meticulous planning and gathering of vital information that paved the way for the mission's triumph.

The aftermath of the Entebbe rescue mission had far-reaching effects on counterterrorism strategies worldwide. This chapter examines how this audacious operation shaped international approaches to combating terrorism and influenced the development of counterterrorism tactics.

The role of international support and cooperation in the success of the rescue mission is explored, underscoring the importance of collective action in the face of adversity.

The media coverage and public perception of the Entebbe hijacking and subsequent rescue are also analyzed, shedding light on the role of the media in shaping public opinion and raising awareness regarding terrorism.

Finally, the subchapter uncovers the stories of the Ugandan hostages, providing a unique perspective on the events at Entebbe from those who experienced them firsthand.

Through meticulous research and firsthand accounts, this subchapter offers a comprehensive analysis of the coordination efforts of the Israeli military during the Entebbe rescue mission. It provides diplomats and historians with invaluable insights into this historical event, its impact on Israeli society, and its enduring legacy in the fight against terrorism.

Mossad's Role in the Rescue Operation

The successful rescue mission at Entebbe stands as a testament to the exceptional capabilities and strategic planning of the Israeli military. At the heart of this operation was Mossad, the renowned Israeli intelligence agency, which played a pivotal role in gathering crucial information and meticulously planning every aspect of the rescue.

Mossad's involvement began even before the hijacking itself, as they closely monitored potential threats and gathered intelligence on various terrorist organizations operating in the region. Their extensive network of informants and agents provided them with valuable insights into the planning and execution of the hijacking.

Once the hijacking occurred, Mossad's focus shifted to gathering real-time intelligence on the hijackers, their demands, and the location of the hostages. Through their covert operations, they were able to infiltrate the ranks of the terrorists, obtaining vital information that would prove critical for the success of the rescue mission.

Mossad's intelligence gathering played a pivotal role in the planning phase of the operation. They provided the Israeli military with accurate blueprints of the Entebbe airport, enabling them to develop a detailed plan for the assault. This level of precision was essential in ensuring the safety of the hostages and the success of the rescue.

Furthermore, Mossad's extensive network of international contacts and diplomatic expertise proved invaluable during the negotiation process. They worked tirelessly behind the scenes, collaborating with various governments and intelligence agencies to secure the release of the hostages. Their diplomatic efforts helped rally international support for the mission and ensured that all necessary resources were made available to the Israeli military.

The successful rescue at Entebbe had far-reaching implications, both domestically and internationally. It was a pivotal moment in Israeli history, serving as a symbol of national pride and unity. The mission showcased the Israeli military's unwavering commitment to protecting its citizens and sent a strong message to terrorists worldwide.

From a global perspective, the Entebbe rescue mission highlighted the importance of international cooperation in combating terrorism. The support and collaboration of various countries were instrumental in the success of the operation. It also served as a wake-up call for governments worldwide, emphasizing the need for robust counterterrorism strategies and cooperation between intelligence agencies.

The role of Mossad in the Entebbe rescue mission remains a shining example of their exceptional capabilities and unwavering commitment to safeguarding Israeli citizens. Their intelligence gathering, strategic planning, and diplomatic efforts were crucial in ensuring the success of the operation. The legacy of Entebbe continues to shape counterterrorism strategies and serves as a reminder of the resilience and determination of the Israeli people in the face of adversity.

Mossad's Contribution to Israeli Intelligence Capabilities

One of the crucial factors that contributed to the success of the Israeli military's heroic rescue mission at Entebbe was the invaluable role played by Mossad, Israel's intelligence agency. Mossad's expertise in gathering information and planning covert operations proved to be instrumental in executing the daring rescue mission.

Mossad's involvement in the Entebbe crisis began immediately after the hijacking of Air France Flight 139. The agency swiftly mobilized its vast network of intelligence assets to gather accurate and up-to-date information on the hijackers, their demands, and the state of the hostages. Through meticulous surveillance and intelligence analysis, Mossad was able to identify the key players involved and their connections to various terrorist organizations.

With this critical information at hand, Mossad collaborated closely with the Israeli military to devise a comprehensive and innovative rescue plan. Mossad's agents infiltrated the airport in Entebbe, Uganda, disguised as airport personnel, to gather intelligence on the layout, security measures, and the location of the hostages. This intelligence proved vital in formulating the rescue strategy and ensuring the element of surprise.

Moreover, Mossad's intelligence capabilities enabled them to anticipate potential obstacles and devise contingency plans. They meticulously studied the behavior and patterns of the Ugandan military and the hijackers, allowing them to accurately predict their responses and adjust their rescue strategy accordingly.

Furthermore, Mossad's expertise in covert operations ensured that the entire rescue mission remained shrouded in secrecy until its execution. Their ability to discreetly gather intelligence without arousing suspicion was crucial in maintaining the element of surprise and preventing any leaks or tip-offs to the hijackers.

The success of the Entebbe rescue mission was a testament to Mossad's unparalleled intelligence capabilities. Their contribution not only saved the lives of the Israeli hostages but also showcased Israel's determination and ability to protect its citizens in the face of terrorism.

Mossad's role in the Entebbe rescue mission marked a milestone in Israeli intelligence capabilities. It demonstrated the agency's ability to gather accurate and timely intelligence, plan complex operations, and execute them with precision. This success further enhanced Mossad's reputation as one of the world's leading intelligence agencies.

In conclusion, Mossad's contribution to Israeli intelligence capabilities played a pivotal role in the success of the Entebbe rescue mission. Their expertise in gathering information, planning covert operations, and maintaining secrecy ensured the safe return of the hostages. This chapter explores the intricate details of Mossad's involvement and its lasting impact on Israeli society, national identity, and counterterrorism strategies. Diplomats and historians will gain a deeper understanding of the historical context, geopolitical implications, and the remarkable achievements of Mossad in this defining moment of Israeli history.

Chapter 7: The Aftermath of the Entebbe Rescue Mission and its Long-Term Effects on Counterterrorism Strategies

The Impact on Global Counterterrorism Efforts

The Entebbe rescue mission, carried out by the Israeli military in 1976, had a profound impact on global counterterrorism efforts. This daring operation, which successfully freed over 100 hostages held captive by Palestinian and German terrorists in Uganda, showcased the Israeli military's exceptional tactical skills, resourcefulness, and determination in combating terrorism. It set a precedent for future counterterrorism operations and influenced the strategies and tactics employed by other nations.

The Entebbe rescue mission highlighted the critical role of the Israeli military in responding to terrorist threats and protecting its citizens. The successful outcome of the operation boosted the morale of the Israeli people and solidified their faith in their military's ability to safeguard their national security. This event became a defining moment for Israeli society, reinforcing their commitment to combating terrorism and defending their homeland.

The rescue mission also underscored the significance of intelligence gathering and planning in counterterrorism operations. The Mossad, Israel's intelligence agency, played a crucial role in providing essential information and insights that enabled the military to execute the operation with precision. This demonstrated the vital role of intelligence agencies in gathering information, analyzing threats, and formulating effective strategies to counter terrorism on a global scale.

The Entebbe rescue mission had far-reaching geopolitical implications, shedding light on the complex dynamics of the Middle East and the global fight against terrorism. It showcased Israel's determination to protect its citizens and highlighted the need for international support and cooperation in combating terrorism. The successful operation garnered significant international attention and support, further solidifying the global community's commitment to fighting terrorism collectively.

Media coverage of the Entebbe hijacking and subsequent rescue played a crucial role in shaping public perception and understanding of terrorism. The dramatic rescue operation captured the world's attention and raised awareness about the grave threat posed by terrorism. This event prompted governments worldwide to reevaluate their counterterrorism strategies and invest in strengthening their intelligence capabilities and special operations forces.

The Entebbe rescue mission also had a lasting impact on the hostages themselves. The personal stories and experiences of the Israeli passengers during their captivity highlighted the resilience, courage, and determination of individuals in the face of extreme adversity. Their stories served as a testament to the strength of the human spirit and inspired others to stand up against terrorism.

In conclusion, the Entebbe rescue mission had a profound impact on global counterterrorism efforts. It showcased the Israeli military's capabilities, emphasized the role of intelligence gathering and planning, and spurred international cooperation in the fight against terrorism. This operation reshaped public perception, influenced counterterrorism strategies, and left a lasting legacy on Israeli society and national identity. The heroic rescue mission at Entebbe remains a pivotal moment in history, reminding us of the ongoing battle against terrorism and the steadfast resolve to protect innocent lives.

Reflections on the Successes and Failures of Operation Thunderbolt

Operation Thunderbolt, the daring rescue mission at Entebbe, stands as a remarkable moment in Israeli military history. As we delve into the successes and failures of this operation, it becomes evident that the Israeli military's unwavering determination and meticulous planning played a pivotal role in its triumph.

The personal stories and experiences of the Israeli passengers during their captivity shed light on the immense courage and resilience they displayed. Their accounts provide a deeper understanding of the psychological and physical challenges they endured, further highlighting the magnitude of their liberation.

Behind the scenes, diplomatic efforts and negotiations were underway to secure the release of the hostages. These diplomatic endeavors underscore the intricate web of relationships and negotiations that played a significant role in the success of Operation Thunderbolt.

The impact of the Entebbe rescue mission on Israeli society and national identity cannot be overstated. This operation served as a symbol of Israeli strength and unity, fostering a sense of national pride and resilience that would endure for years to come.

Examining the historical context and geopolitical implications of the hijacking and rescue operation reveals the complex dynamics at play. The audacity of the hijackers and the swift response by the Israeli military showcased the ever-present threat of terrorism and the necessity for proactive counterterrorism measures.

Central to the success of Operation Thunderbolt was the role of Mossad, the Israeli intelligence agency. Their meticulous gathering of information and strategic planning formed the backbone of the operation, illustrating the vital importance of intelligence agencies in combating terrorism.

While Operation Thunderbolt was undoubtedly a triumph, its aftermath warrants examination. Exploring the long-term effects on counterterrorism strategies allows us to gauge the lasting impact of this mission and its implications for future operations.

International support and cooperation were crucial to the success of the rescue mission. Understanding the role played by various nations and their collaboration provides a comprehensive view of the global response to this crisis.

Media coverage and public perception of the Entebbe hijacking and subsequent rescue shaped the narrative and influenced public opinion. Analyzing the media's portrayal of these events allows us to unpack the power and influence of the press in shaping public discourse.

Lastly, exploring the stories and perspectives of the Ugandan hostages offers a unique vantage point. Their ordeal and their reflections provide valuable insights into the events at Entebbe from a different lens.

In conclusion, Operation Thunderbolt's successes and failures leave an indelible mark on history. By examining its various facets, we gain a deeper understanding of the Israeli military's role, the experiences of those involved, the diplomatic efforts, and the wider implications. As diplomats and historians, it is our duty to preserve these reflections and ensure that the lessons learned from Operation Thunderbolt continue to shape our understanding of counterterrorism efforts.

The Evolution of Hostage Rescue Techniques

In the subchapter titled "The Evolution of Hostage Rescue Techniques," we delve into the remarkable advancements made by the Israeli military in the field of hostage rescue operations. This chapter explores the historical context, geopolitical implications, and the impact of the Entebbe rescue mission on Israeli society and national identity.

The rescue mission at Entebbe in 1976 was a pivotal moment in the history of hostage rescue techniques. The Israeli military showcased its unparalleled capabilities, which revolutionized the way such operations were conducted worldwide.

The chapter begins by examining the role of the Israeli military and how they meticulously planned and executed the rescue mission. We discuss the personal stories and experiences of the Israeli passengers during their captivity, highlighting their courage and resilience. Through their narratives, we gain a deeper understanding of the psychological and physical challenges they faced.

Simultaneously, we shed light on the diplomatic efforts and negotiations that unfolded behind the scenes to secure the release of the hostages. Diplomats and historians will appreciate the intricate details of the negotiations, the challenges faced, and the international support that played a significant role in the success of the mission.

The involvement of Mossad, the Israeli intelligence agency, is also explored in this subchapter. We delve into their crucial role in gathering information and planning the rescue mission. Readers will gain insights into Mossad's intelligence-gathering techniques, which were instrumental in the success of the operation.

Moreover, the aftermath of the Entebbe rescue mission and its long-term effects on counterterrorism strategies are discussed. We analyze the impact of this operation on Israeli society and national identity, as well as its influence on global counterterrorism measures.

The chapter also provides a comprehensive analysis of the media coverage and public perception of the Entebbe hijacking and subsequent rescue. Through an exploration of different perspectives, diplomats and historians can gain a more nuanced understanding of the events and their portrayal in the media.

Finally, we shed light on the stories of the Ugandan hostages, presenting their unique perspective on the events at Entebbe. Their narratives offer a contrasting viewpoint, enabling readers to comprehend the complex dynamics at play during the rescue mission.

By delving into these diverse aspects, this subchapter aims to provide diplomats and historians with a comprehensive understanding of the evolution of hostage rescue techniques, the geopolitical implications, and the long-lasting impact of the Entebbe rescue mission.

Entebbe's Influence on Counterterrorism Training and Special Forces Operations

The Entebbe rescue mission, also known as Operation Thunderbolt, was a pivotal moment in the history of counterterrorism and special forces operations. This subchapter explores the profound impact of this daring operation on various aspects of military and security strategies, as well as its wider implications on Israeli society, national identity, and international cooperation.

The Israeli military's role in the Entebbe rescue mission was nothing short of extraordinary. Diplomats and historians will be fascinated by the meticulous planning, precise execution, and audaciousness displayed by the Israeli special forces during this operation. This subchapter delves into the tactics, training, and equipment utilized by the Israeli military, providing valuable insights into modern counterterrorism strategies and the evolution of special forces operations.

Furthermore, the personal stories and experiences of the Israeli passengers held captive during their ordeal shed light on the resilience and determination of the human spirit. Their accounts offer a unique perspective on the psychological impact of captivity and the unwavering commitment to survival. These narratives appeal to diplomats and historians interested in the human aspect of conflict and resilience in the face of adversity.

Behind the scenes, diplomatic efforts and negotiations played a crucial role in securing the release of the hostages. This subchapter explores the intricate web of negotiations, the role of international actors, and the delicate balance between political considerations and the imperative to save lives. It provides an in-depth analysis of the diplomatic complexities involved in such high-stakes situations.

The Entebbe rescue mission also had profound implications for Israeli society and national identity. The successful operation became a symbol of Israel's unwavering commitment to the safety and security of its citizens. It bolstered national pride and forged a collective identity rooted in resilience and determination. This subchapter examines the long-lasting effects of the mission on Israel's national psyche and the shaping of its security policies.

Moreover, the historical context and geopolitical implications of the hijacking and rescue operation are explored in detail. This includes an analysis of the regional dynamics, the threat posed by international terrorism, and the broader implications for global security. It provides a comprehensive assessment of the impact of this mission on the international stage.

The critical role played by Mossad, Israel's intelligence agency, in gathering information and planning the rescue mission is also thoroughly examined. This subchapter delves into the intelligence-gathering techniques employed by Mossad and the significance of actionable intelligence in successful counterterrorism operations.

Lastly, the aftermath of the Entebbe rescue mission and its long-term effects on counterterrorism strategies are discussed. This includes an assessment of how the operation influenced the development of international cooperation and support in combating terrorism. It also analyzes the changes in counterterrorism tactics and strategies that were implemented in the wake of the mission's success.

In conclusion, this subchapter provides a comprehensive exploration of the Entebbe rescue mission's influence on counterterrorism training and special forces operations. It delves into the personal stories, diplomatic efforts, geopolitical implications, intelligence gathering, and long-term effects of this historic operation. Diplomats and historians will find this subchapter invaluable in understanding the multifaceted impact of Entebbe on various aspects of military operations, national identity, and international cooperation in the fight against terrorism.

Evaluating the Legacy of Entebbe in the Modern Era

The daring rescue mission carried out by the Israeli military at Entebbe Airport in 1976 remains a significant event in history, with far-reaching implications for the world. In this subchapter, "Evaluating the Legacy of Entebbe in the Modern Era," we delve into the multifaceted aspects of this operation, examining its impact on Israeli society, its geopolitical implications, and its long-term effects on counterterrorism strategies.

One of the key focuses of this subchapter is the role of the Israeli military in the rescue mission at Entebbe. We explore the meticulous planning and execution of the operation, highlighting the bravery and skill of the Israeli soldiers involved. By analyzing their tactics and strategies, we gain valuable insights into the military's crucial role in successfully rescuing the hostages.

Additionally, we delve into the personal stories and experiences of the Israeli passengers during their captivity. By recounting their accounts, we provide a poignant and human perspective on the traumatic ordeal they endured. These narratives offer a deeper understanding of the resilience and determination displayed by the hostages in the face of adversity.

Furthermore, we shed light on the diplomatic efforts and negotiations behind the scenes to secure the release of the hostages. By examining the intricate web of international diplomacy, we uncover the delicate balance of power and the intricate negotiations that took place to ensure a successful outcome.

The Entebbe rescue mission also had a profound impact on Israeli society and national identity. We analyze how this event became a defining moment in Israeli history, shaping the nation's perception of itself and its role in the world. We explore how the successful operation boosted national morale and bolstered Israel's standing in the international community.

Moreover, we delve into the historical context and geopolitical implications of the hijacking and rescue operation. By examining the complex web of regional and global dynamics, we gain a comprehensive understanding of the event's significance within the broader geopolitical landscape of the time.

In addition, we highlight the role of Mossad, the Israeli intelligence agency, in gathering information and planning the rescue mission. By delving into the agency's covert operations, we unravel the intricate intelligence network that facilitated the success of the mission.

Furthermore, we explore the aftermath of the Entebbe rescue mission and its long-term effects on counterterrorism strategies. By analyzing the response of governments worldwide, we evaluate how this operation influenced future counterterrorism efforts and shaped international cooperation in combating terrorism.

We also examine the role of international support and cooperation in the success of the rescue mission. By highlighting the contributions of nations and organizations that rallied behind Israel, we underscore the importance of collaboration in achieving a common goal.

Additionally, we explore the media coverage and public perception of the Entebbe hijacking and subsequent rescue. By analyzing how the event was portrayed in the media and its impact on public opinion, we gain insights into the power of media narratives in shaping historical events.

Lastly, we shed light on the stories of the Ugandan hostages and their perspective on the events at Entebbe. By giving voice to their experiences, we provide a comprehensive and inclusive narrative that encompasses the perspectives of all those affected by this momentous event.

In conclusion, this subchapter offers a comprehensive evaluation of the legacy of Entebbe in the modern era. By exploring various aspects of the operation, we provide a nuanced understanding of its significance and its enduring impact on diplomacy, national identity, counterterrorism strategies, and public perception.

Chapter 8: The Role of International Support and Cooperation in the Success of the Rescue Mission

Israeli Diplomatic Efforts to Garner International Support

In the face of the Entebbe hijacking crisis, the Israeli government launched a series of diplomatic efforts to garner international support and secure the safe release of the hostages. These efforts played a crucial role in the success of the daring rescue mission and showcased Israel's diplomatic prowess on the international stage.

Israeli diplomats utilized their global network to rally support from key allies and international organizations. They engaged in intense negotiations with governments across the world, urging them to take a firm stance against terrorism and support Israel in its fight against the hijackers. Diplomatic channels were activated, and Israeli envoys tirelessly worked to build alliances and secure the backing of influential nations.

One of the main challenges faced by Israeli diplomats was overcoming the reluctance of some countries to support a military operation on foreign soil. They emphasized the urgency of the situation and highlighted the violation of international law by the hijackers. Israeli diplomats skillfully presented a case that justified the use of force as a last resort to protect innocent lives.

The diplomatic efforts also involved leveraging Israel's intelligence capabilities, particularly the Mossad. Israeli intelligence agents gathered crucial information about the hijackers, their motives, and their connections. This intelligence was shared with partner nations, enhancing their understanding of the threat and helping to build consensus for action.

The success of the diplomatic campaign was evident in the strong international support that Israel received. Numerous countries expressed solidarity and offered assistance, both publicly and behind closed doors. The United States, in particular, played a significant role, offering logistical support and intelligence cooperation. This collaboration highlighted the strong bond between the two nations and their shared commitment to fighting terrorism.

The international media played a crucial role in shaping public opinion and putting pressure on the hijackers. The Israeli government employed its diplomatic channels to ensure that the media coverage portrayed the hijackers as terrorists and the rescue mission as a heroic act of self-defense. This portrayal helped galvanize public support and generate international outrage against the hijackers.

The diplomatic efforts ultimately led to the successful rescue of the hostages, with only a minimal loss of life. The operation showcased Israel's determination and capability to protect its citizens, enhancing its national identity and pride. It also had far-reaching implications for counterterrorism strategies worldwide, demonstrating the need for decisive action and international cooperation in the face of terrorism.

The Entebbe rescue mission remains a defining moment in Israeli history, illustrating the resilience of its people and their commitment to protecting innocent lives. The diplomatic efforts that accompanied the mission highlighted Israel's ability to navigate complex international relations and garner support for its cause. This chapter explores the behind-the-scenes negotiations, alliances, and diplomatic triumphs that paved the way for the historic rescue operation. It sheds light on the role of international cooperation, the impact on counterterrorism strategies, and the enduring legacy of the Entebbe rescue mission.

Collaboration with Allied Intelligence Agencies

One crucial aspect of the Entebbe rescue mission was the collaboration between the Israeli military and various allied intelligence agencies. This subchapter delves into the intricate web of international cooperation that played a significant role in the success of the mission.

The Israeli military, in close coordination with Mossad, the renowned Israeli intelligence agency, leveraged their extensive networks to gather vital information regarding the hijacking. Mossad's intelligence-gathering capabilities were instrumental in identifying the hijackers and understanding their motives, aiding in the planning of the rescue mission.

Additionally, the collaboration with allied intelligence agencies provided crucial support to the Israeli military. Intelligence sharing and joint efforts with agencies from countries such as the United States, Germany, and Kenya allowed for a comprehensive understanding of the situation at Entebbe. The collective intelligence helped in formulating effective strategies and ensuring the safety of the hostages during the operation.

Moreover, the diplomatic efforts behind the scenes were closely intertwined with intelligence cooperation. Diplomats and intelligence officials worked hand in hand to negotiate with Ugandan President Idi Amin and secure the release of the hostages. This delicate diplomatic dance required close collaboration between Israeli and foreign intelligence agencies, as they shared critical information and strategies to exert maximum pressure on Amin and the hijackers.

The success of the Entebbe rescue mission highlighted the significance of international support and cooperation in countering terrorism. The united front presented by various countries showcased the strength of collaborative efforts against acts of terror. This event served as an important turning point in counterterrorism strategies, emphasizing the need for intelligence cooperation and joint operations to combat global threats effectively.

The impact of the Entebbe rescue mission extended far beyond the immediate aftermath. It not only solidified Israeli society's belief in the strength of their military and intelligence agencies but also bolstered their national identity. The successful operation became a symbol of Israeli resilience and determination, shaping the nation's perception of itself as a formidable force capable of protecting its citizens both domestically and abroad.

In conclusion, the collaboration with allied intelligence agencies was a critical component of the Entebbe rescue mission. The joint intelligence efforts, diplomatic negotiations, and collective support showcased the power of international cooperation in countering terrorism. The success of the mission not only had a profound impact on Israeli society but also left a lasting legacy in terms of counterterrorism strategies worldwide.

The Role of International Military Assistance

In the book "Entebbe Unveiled: The Israeli Military's Heroic Rescue Mission," the subchapter "The Role of International Military Assistance" delves into the crucial support received from various countries during the daring rescue mission at Entebbe. This chapter aims to provide diplomats and historians with a comprehensive understanding of the collaborative efforts that helped ensure the successful liberation of the hostages.

The Israeli military's rescue operation at Entebbe Airport in Uganda was an audacious and high-stakes mission, requiring meticulous planning and precise execution. However, the task would not have been possible without the invaluable assistance provided by international partners. The chapter highlights the significance of this support in achieving the mission's objectives.

From the onset, the Israeli government sought international cooperation to maximize the chances of success. They reached out to allies and sympathetic nations, seeking their assistance in various aspects of the mission. The chapter explores the specific contributions made by different countries, such as providing intelligence, logistical support, and military expertise.

International intelligence agencies played a crucial role in gathering information about the hijackers, the hostages' location, and the airport's layout. The cooperation between Israeli intelligence agency Mossad and its foreign counterparts was pivotal in formulating a comprehensive rescue plan. The subchapter examines the coordination between these agencies and the intelligence breakthroughs that paved the way for the successful operation.

Moreover, the chapter delves into the military assistance offered by selected nations. Some countries provided vital resources, such as aircraft, to transport the Israeli commandos and their equipment to Entebbe. Others offered their military expertise and advice, contributing to the meticulous planning and tactical execution of the rescue.

Furthermore, the subchapter explores the diplomatic efforts undertaken behind the scenes to secure the release of the hostages. Israeli diplomats engaged in intense negotiations with Ugandan authorities, seeking a peaceful resolution while simultaneously preparing for a military operation. The international community also played a significant role in exerting diplomatic pressure on Uganda and the hijackers, ultimately influencing the outcome of the crisis.

The collaboration between Israel and its international partners had far-reaching implications. It not only highlighted the importance of international support and cooperation in counterterrorism efforts but also showcased Israel's ability to garner global assistance during times of crisis. The chapter analyzes the impact of this successful mission on Israeli society, national identity, and the development of future counterterrorism strategies.

In conclusion, the subchapter "The Role of International Military Assistance" provides diplomats and historians with a comprehensive account of the collaborative efforts that were instrumental in the success of the Entebbe rescue mission. It highlights the invaluable contributions made by international partners, ranging from intelligence gathering and logistical support to diplomatic negotiations. This chapter sheds light on the historical context, geopolitical implications, and long-term effects of the mission while underscoring the importance of international cooperation in counterterrorism operations.

The Significance of International Unity in Counterterrorism Efforts

In the fight against terrorism, international unity plays a crucial role in ensuring the success of counterterrorism efforts. Nowhere is this more evident than in the heroic rescue mission carried out by the Israeli military at Entebbe. This subchapter explores the significance of international unity in the context of this historic event, addressing diplomats and historians who are interested in gaining a comprehensive understanding of the multifaceted aspects surrounding the operation.

The Entebbe rescue mission was a testament to the unwavering determination and bravery of the Israeli military. However, it also highlighted the importance of international support and cooperation. The Israeli government, recognizing the need for a united front, sought assistance from various countries, fostering alliances and collaboration. Diplomatic efforts and negotiations behind the scenes were instrumental in securing the release of the hostages. This subchapter delves into the intricate web of diplomatic maneuvers and the pivotal role they played in the success of the mission.

Moreover, the Entebbe rescue had far-reaching implications on Israeli society and national identity. The audacious operation not only bolstered national pride but also reshaped the perception of Israel's military capabilities. This subchapter analyzes the impact of the mission on Israeli society, exploring how it became a symbol of resilience and determination.

To fully comprehend the historical context and geopolitical implications of the hijacking and rescue operation, it is essential to examine the role of Mossad, Israel's intelligence agency. This subchapter sheds light on the agency's meticulous gathering of information and strategic planning, showcasing its pivotal contribution to the mission's success.

Examining the aftermath of the Entebbe rescue mission provides valuable insights into the long-term effects on counterterrorism strategies. The operation served as a turning point, prompting nations worldwide to reevaluate their approach to combating terrorism. This subchapter explores how the mission influenced counterterrorism strategies globally, emphasizing the need for international collaboration.

Furthermore, the media coverage and public perception of the Entebbe hijacking and subsequent rescue shaped the narrative surrounding the event. This subchapter delves into the media's portrayal of the operation and its impact on public opinion, highlighting the importance of accurate and responsible reporting.

The perspectives of the Ugandan hostages offer a unique vantage point, shedding light on the experiences and emotions of those held captive during the crisis. This subchapter provides a platform for their stories, giving voice to the victims and offering a comprehensive understanding of the events at Entebbe.

In conclusion, international unity serves as a linchpin in counterterrorism efforts. The Entebbe rescue mission exemplifies the significance of global cooperation, and this subchapter aims to provide diplomats and historians with a comprehensive analysis of the role of international support, diplomatic negotiations, and the long-term effects of the operation. By examining various perspectives, from the Israeli military to the Ugandan hostages, a holistic understanding of the events at Entebbe is achieved.

Lessons Learned for Future International Cooperation

The Entebbe rescue mission was a defining moment in history that showcased the Israeli military's extraordinary courage and ability to execute a complex operation. However, the success of this mission was not solely attributed to the Israeli military's prowess, but also to the invaluable lessons learned from the entire process. These lessons are not only significant in understanding the dynamics of hostage situations but also in shaping future international cooperation.

Firstly, the role of the Israeli military in the rescue mission at Entebbe highlighted the importance of meticulous planning and coordination. The military's ability to adapt to unforeseen circumstances and swiftly execute their plan was crucial in achieving their objectives. This experience serves as a reminder that in any international crisis, meticulous planning and coordination among different agencies and countries are essential for success.

Secondly, the personal stories and experiences of the Israeli passengers during their captivity shed light on the psychological resilience required in hostage situations. The ability to maintain a sense of hope and unity among hostages is a valuable lesson that can be applied in future hostage negotiation scenarios.

Additionally, the diplomatic efforts and negotiations behind the scenes to secure the release of the hostages demonstrated the significance of international cooperation. The collaboration between Israel and other countries, including Kenya and the United States, played a vital role in the mission's success. This experience emphasizes the importance of building strong diplomatic alliances and partnerships in times of crisis.

Moreover, the impact of the Entebbe rescue mission on Israeli society and national identity is a testament to the power of unity and solidarity. The mission instilled a sense of pride and resilience in the Israeli people, shaping their national identity and strengthening their determination to combat terrorism.

Furthermore, the historical context and geopolitical implications of the hijacking and rescue operation highlight the need for a comprehensive understanding of regional dynamics in counterterrorism strategies. This experience serves as a reminder that successful counterterrorism efforts must consider the underlying causes and complexities of the situation.

In conclusion, the Entebbe rescue mission offers valuable lessons for future international cooperation. Meticulous planning, psychological resilience, diplomatic collaboration, national unity, and an understanding of regional dynamics are crucial elements in achieving success in hostage situations and counterterrorism efforts. By analyzing and implementing these lessons, diplomats and historians can work towards a safer and more secure world.

Chapter 9: The Media Coverage and Public Perception of the Entebbe Hijacking and Subsequent Rescue

Initial Media Coverage and International Attention

The hijacking of Air France Flight 139 on June 27, 1976, and the subsequent rescue mission at Entebbe Airport captivated the world's attention and garnered extensive media coverage. This subchapter explores the immediate response of the international community and the media to these unprecedented events.

As news of the hijacking broke, headlines across the globe focused on the audacity of the terrorists and the plight of the Israeli passengers held hostage in Uganda. Diplomats and historians alike will find this section particularly enlightening as it delves into the role of the Israeli military in planning and executing the daring rescue mission.

Furthermore, the personal stories and experiences of the Israeli passengers during their harrowing captivity shed light on the resilience and bravery they displayed in the face of extreme adversity. This subchapter offers a unique perspective on their ordeal, giving diplomats and historians invaluable insights into the human aspect of this high-stakes operation.

Behind the scenes, intense diplomatic efforts and negotiations were underway to secure the release of the hostages. This subchapter uncovers the intricate web of diplomatic maneuverings and the role various nations played in facilitating the success of the rescue mission.

The impact of the Entebbe operation on Israeli society and national identity cannot be overstated. This section delves into the profound effect it had on the collective psyche of the nation, shaping Israeli perceptions of resilience, courage, and the necessity of safeguarding their people at all costs.

Examining the historical context and geopolitical implications of the hijacking and rescue operation provides valuable insights into the complex dynamics of the era. Diplomats and historians will gain a comprehensive understanding of the regional tensions, global power dynamics, and the intricate web of alliances that shaped both the hijacking and the subsequent rescue mission.

Central to the success of the rescue operation was the meticulous planning and intelligence-gathering by the Mossad, the Israeli intelligence agency. This subchapter unveils the fascinating details surrounding Mossad's involvement, shedding light on their crucial role in securing the freedom of the hostages.

The aftermath of the Entebbe operation had far-reaching consequences for counterterrorism strategies worldwide. This section explores the long-term effects of the mission on international efforts to combat terrorism, providing diplomats and historians with an invaluable perspective on the strategic implications of this landmark event.

The role of international support and cooperation in the success of the rescue mission is also examined. The subchapter underscores the importance of collaborative efforts between nations and showcases the power of global solidarity in achieving seemingly impossible goals.

Finally, the media coverage and public perception of the Entebbe hijacking and subsequent rescue provide a fascinating glimpse into the intersection of journalism and politics. This section analyzes the media's portrayal of the events and its influence on public opinion, offering diplomats and historians a unique perspective on the power of the media in shaping public discourse.

In addition to the Israeli perspective, this subchapter also delves into the stories of the Ugandan hostages and their perspective on the events at Entebbe. By including their voices, diplomats and historians gain a more comprehensive understanding of the complex dynamics at play during this tumultuous period.

Overall, this subchapter provides a comprehensive exploration of the initial media coverage and international attention surrounding the hijacking and rescue mission at Entebbe. Its multidimensional approach appeals to both diplomats and historians, offering a nuanced understanding of this transformative event in history.

Shaping the Narrative: Israeli and Ugandan Perspectives

The subchapter "Shaping the Narrative: Israeli and Ugandan Perspectives" delves into the intricate details of the Entebbe rescue mission, providing a comprehensive analysis of the Israeli and Ugandan viewpoints surrounding this historic event. Addressed to diplomats and historians, this section seeks to shed light on the various dimensions of the mission, ranging from personal stories of the Israeli passengers to the impact on Israeli society and national identity. Furthermore, it explores the historical context, geopolitical implications, diplomatic efforts, and the role of Mossad in planning the rescue.

One of the central focuses of this subchapter is the role of the Israeli military in the Entebbe rescue mission. By examining the operational details and strategies employed by the Israeli Defense Forces (IDF), readers gain insight into the immense bravery and determination displayed by the Israeli soldiers involved. This analysis is complemented by a collection of personal stories and experiences of the Israeli passengers during their captivity, highlighting their resilience and courage in the face of adversity.

To provide a holistic understanding of the situation, this subchapter also delves into the diplomatic efforts and negotiations that unfolded behind the scenes to secure the release of the hostages. By exploring the intricate web of international relationships and the delicate balance of power, readers gain a deeper appreciation for the complexities involved in resolving such a crisis.

The impact of the Entebbe rescue mission on Israeli society and national identity is another crucial aspect explored in this subchapter. By analyzing the aftermath of the mission, readers witness the profound effects it had on Israel's counterterrorism strategies and its perception of itself as a nation. Moreover, the subchapter delves into the media coverage and public perception of the hijacking and subsequent rescue, shedding light on how the events were portrayed and understood by the international community.

While the Israeli perspective forms the backbone of this subchapter, it also strives to include the stories and perspectives of the Ugandan hostages. By exploring their experiences, readers gain a more nuanced understanding of the events at Entebbe and the impact it had on the local population.

Overall, "Shaping the Narrative: Israeli and Ugandan Perspectives" presents a comprehensive analysis of the Entebbe rescue mission, catering to the interests of diplomats and historians alike. By exploring the various dimensions of this historic event, the subchapter provides a rich tapestry of information that contributes to our collective knowledge of the mission and its far-reaching implications.

Impact on Public Opinion and Global Awareness

The Entebbe rescue mission, carried out by the Israeli military in 1976, had a profound impact on public opinion and global awareness. This subchapter delves into the various aspects that contributed to this impact, examining the role of the Israeli military, the personal stories of the Israeli passengers, the diplomatic efforts behind the scenes, the impact on Israeli society and national identity, the historical context and geopolitical implications, the role of Mossad, the aftermath and long-term effects on counterterrorism strategies, international support and cooperation, media coverage, and the perspectives of the Ugandan hostages.

The daring and successful rescue mission by the Israeli military showcased their exceptional capabilities and reaffirmed their reputation as a formidable force. The meticulous planning and execution of the operation solidified their role as a global leader in counterterrorism. Diplomats and historians will gain valuable insights into the operation, including the strategies employed and the challenges faced by the Israeli military.

Through firsthand accounts, readers will discover the harrowing experiences of the Israeli passengers during their captivity. These personal stories shed light on the resilience, courage, and determination displayed by the hostages, highlighting their unwavering spirit in the face of adversity.

Behind the scenes, diplomatic efforts and negotiations were underway to secure the release of the hostages. This subchapter examines the intricate web of negotiations, involving various international actors, that ultimately led to the successful resolution of the crisis. The diplomatic intricacies and the delicate balance of power at play will provide diplomats and historians with a comprehensive understanding of the intricate negotiations that took place.

The impact of the Entebbe rescue mission on Israeli society and national identity cannot be overstated. The subchapter explores the profound effect the operation had on Israeli society, fueling a sense of national pride and solidarity. The mission's success became a symbol of Israeli resilience and determination, shaping the country's collective memory and national narrative.

Furthermore, this subchapter delves into the historical context and geopolitical implications of the hijacking and rescue operation. By examining the regional dynamics and the global response to the crisis, diplomats and historians will gain a broader perspective on the event's significance in the context of the Cold War and the Israeli-Arab conflict.

The role of Mossad, the Israeli intelligence agency, in gathering information and planning the rescue mission is also explored. This subchapter reveals the meticulous intelligence gathering and operational planning that enabled the Israeli military to execute the mission with precision.

The aftermath of the Entebbe rescue mission and its long-term effects on counterterrorism strategies are examined in detail. This subchapter analyzes how the operation served as a turning point in counterterrorism tactics, influencing the development of future strategies and operations worldwide.

International support and cooperation played a crucial role in the success of the rescue mission. By exploring the extent of international collaboration, diplomats and historians will gain insights into the significance of global solidarity in combating terrorism.

The media coverage and public perception of the Entebbe hijacking and subsequent rescue are also analyzed. This subchapter delves into the media's portrayal of the event, its impact on public opinion, and the lasting impressions it left on global consciousness.

Finally, the subchapter addresses the stories and perspectives of the Ugandan hostages. By examining their experiences and their viewpoints on the events at Entebbe, a more comprehensive and nuanced understanding of the crisis is attained.

Overall, this subchapter provides a comprehensive analysis of the impact of the Entebbe rescue mission on public opinion and global awareness. It explores the multifaceted dimensions of the operation, addressing the interests of diplomats and historians alike.

Media Ethics and Responsibility in Reporting Hostage Situations

The media plays a crucial role in shaping public perception and understanding of significant events such as hostage situations. In the case of the Entebbe rescue mission, the media's coverage and reporting of the hijacking and subsequent rescue had far-reaching implications for the hostages, the Israeli military, and international diplomacy. This subchapter delves into the ethical considerations and responsibilities that journalists and media organizations face when reporting on hostage situations, with a specific focus on the Entebbe rescue mission.

One of the primary challenges faced by the media in reporting hostage situations is balancing the public's right to information with the safety and well-being of the hostages. The Israeli military, in this case, had to carefully consider how much information to disclose to the media to avoid jeopardizing the rescue operation. Journalists, on the other hand, had to navigate the fine line between reporting the facts and not inadvertently aiding the hijackers or compromising the safety of the hostages.

The subchapter also explores the ethical dilemmas faced by journalists in obtaining information and interviews from the hostages. While their personal stories and experiences are crucial for providing a comprehensive account of the events, journalists must ensure that the survivors' privacy and emotional well-being are respected. Sensationalizing or exploiting their trauma for the sake of ratings or headlines is not only ethically questionable but also undermines the credibility and integrity of the media.

Furthermore, the subchapter discusses the media's responsibility in accurately portraying the diplomatic efforts and negotiations behind the scenes. Journalists have a duty to provide the public with a balanced and unbiased account of the negotiations, avoiding sensationalism or misrepresentation that could hinder the diplomatic process or mislead the audience.

Additionally, the subchapter examines the media's role in shaping public perception and national identity. The coverage of the Entebbe rescue mission had a profound impact on Israeli society, bolstering national pride and cementing the Israeli military's reputation as a formidable force in counterterrorism. Understanding the media's influence on public opinion allows diplomats and historians to analyze the long-term effects of the rescue mission on counterterrorism strategies and national security.

Overall, this subchapter on media ethics and responsibility in reporting hostage situations provides diplomats and historians with critical insights into the challenges faced by journalists, the impact of media coverage on public perception, and the ethical considerations that must be upheld in such situations. By examining the media's role in the Entebbe rescue mission, readers gain a deeper understanding of the historical context, geopolitical implications, and the stories of the hostages involved in these high-stakes events.

The Legacy of Entebbe in Media Representation of Terrorism

In the subchapter titled "The Legacy of Entebbe in Media Representation of Terrorism," we delve into the profound impact that the Entebbe rescue mission had on the portrayal of terrorism in the media. This chapter analyzes the significant role of the Israeli military in the rescue mission at Entebbe, the personal stories and experiences of the Israeli passengers during their captivity, and the diplomatic efforts and negotiations behind the scenes to secure the release of the hostages.

The daring rescue mission at Entebbe not only showcased the remarkable courage and skill of the Israeli military but also had a lasting impact on Israeli society and national identity. This chapter explores the profound effects of the Entebbe rescue mission on the collective psyche of the Israeli people, highlighting how it bolstered their resilience and determination in the face of terrorism.

Furthermore, the historical context and geopolitical implications of the hijacking and rescue operation are examined, shedding light on the complex dynamics that surrounded this event. The role of Mossad, the Israeli intelligence agency, in gathering crucial information and meticulously planning the rescue mission is also discussed, showcasing their instrumental contribution to the success of the operation.

We also explore the aftermath of the Entebbe rescue mission and its long-term effects on counterterrorism strategies. The lessons learned from this operation played a pivotal role in shaping future approaches to combating terrorism, both domestically and internationally.

Additionally, this subchapter delves into the media coverage and public perception of the Entebbe hijacking and subsequent rescue. It examines how the media portrayed the events at Entebbe and the impact it had on shaping public opinion and understanding of terrorism.

Lastly, we shed light on the stories of the Ugandan hostages and their unique perspectives on the events at Entebbe. Their experiences offer a critical lens through which we can understand the human toll of terrorism and the enduring trauma faced by those directly affected.

In conclusion, this subchapter provides diplomats and historians with a comprehensive analysis of the legacy of Entebbe in media representation of terrorism. By examining various facets such as the role of the Israeli military, personal stories of the hostages, diplomatic efforts, and media coverage, we gain a deeper understanding of the broader implications and lasting effects of this historic event.

Chapter 10: The Stories of the Ugandan Hostages and their Perspective on the Events at Entebbe

The Ugandan Hostages: Victims Caught in the Middle

In the subchapter "The Ugandan Hostages: Victims Caught in the Middle," we delve into the harrowing experiences of the innocent victims who found themselves at the mercy of terrorists during the infamous hijacking at Entebbe. This section of "Entebbe Unveiled: The Israeli Military's Heroic Rescue Mission" aims to shed light on the personal stories and perspectives of the hostages, providing a comprehensive understanding of their plight.

Through meticulous research and interviews, this subchapter offers a detailed account of the Israeli passengers' experiences during their captivity. It explores the emotional and physical toll they endured, the fears they faced, and the resilience they displayed while held hostage in Uganda. By delving into their personal narratives, we aim to provide a humanizing perspective on the events at Entebbe, allowing readers to empathize with the victims and gain a deeper understanding of the trauma they endured.

Furthermore, this subchapter also examines the diplomatic efforts and negotiations that took place behind the scenes to secure the release of the hostages. It highlights the intricate diplomatic maneuvering, the delicate balance of power, and the international cooperation that ultimately played a pivotal role in the successful outcome of the rescue mission. By delving into the historical context and geopolitical implications of the hijacking and rescue operation, we provide diplomats and historians with valuable insights into the intricacies of international diplomacy during times of crisis.

Moreover, we explore the long-term effects of the Entebbe rescue mission on Israeli society and national identity. This subchapter analyzes how the successful operation not only bolstered Israeli morale but also shaped future counterterrorism strategies. It examines the role of the Israeli intelligence agency, Mossad, in gathering information and planning the rescue mission, emphasizing their vital contribution to the operation's success.

Additionally, this subchapter investigates the media coverage and public perception of the Entebbe hijacking and subsequent rescue. By analyzing the way these events were portrayed in the media, we provide an insight into how they were perceived by both domestic and international audiences. Moreover, we explore the impact of international support and cooperation on the success of the rescue mission, highlighting the significance of collective action in times of crisis.

Finally, this subchapter offers a platform for the Ugandan hostages to share their stories and perspectives on the events at Entebbe. By amplifying their voices, we uncover the human side of this tragedy, shedding light on the experiences, emotions, and perspectives of those caught in the middle. Through their stories, readers gain a comprehensive understanding of the full scope of this multifaceted event.

Overall, "The Ugandan Hostages: Victims Caught in the Middle" subchapter provides diplomats and historians with a nuanced exploration of the personal, diplomatic, and historical aspects of the Entebbe hijacking and rescue mission. By delving into these various niches, this subchapter aims to offer a comprehensive account that contributes to a deeper understanding of this pivotal moment in history.

Experiences of Fear, Survival, and Trauma

In this subchapter, titled "Experiences of Fear, Survival, and Trauma," we delve into the gripping personal stories of the Israeli passengers who were held captive during the infamous Entebbe hijacking. Addressing a distinguished audience of diplomats and historians, we explore the multifaceted aspects of this dramatic event that captivated the world.

Through exclusive interviews and previously untold accounts, we shed light on the harrowing experiences of the Israeli hostages during their captivity. Their stories depict the sheer terror they faced, the resilience they displayed, and the emotional trauma that lingered long after their release. These personal narratives offer a profound insight into the human spirit's capacity to endure extreme adversity.

Furthermore, we uncover the intricate diplomatic efforts and negotiations that took place behind the scenes to secure the release of the hostages. This section highlights the delicate balance between political maneuvering and the preservation of human lives, shedding light on the immense pressure faced by those involved in the rescue mission.

We also examine the profound impact of the Entebbe rescue mission on Israeli society and national identity. The audacious operation, executed by the Israeli military, engendered a sense of national pride and unity, as it showcased the unwavering commitment of the nation to protect its citizens at all costs.

To provide a comprehensive understanding, we analyze the historical context and geopolitical implications of the hijacking and rescue operation. The intricate web of global politics and alliances during this period is unravelled, illustrating the significance of the Entebbe mission within the broader international landscape.

Central to this narrative is the role of Mossad, the Israeli intelligence agency, in gathering critical information and meticulously planning the rescue mission. We delve into the agency's remarkable efforts, highlighting their invaluable contribution to the success of the operation.

Moreover, we explore the aftermath of the Entebbe rescue mission and its long-term effects on counterterrorism strategies. The daring operation set a precedent for future counterterrorism operations worldwide, influencing tactics and approaches in the fight against terrorism.

The role of international support and cooperation in the success of the rescue mission is also examined. We discuss the collaborative efforts of various nations, highlighting the significance of global solidarity in times of crisis.

Additionally, we delve into the media coverage and public perception of the Entebbe hijacking and subsequent rescue. We explore how the media shaped public opinion and how the world reacted to this audacious act of terrorism and the subsequent military response.

Finally, we shed light on the stories of the Ugandan hostages and their unique perspective on the events at Entebbe. By providing a comprehensive account of their experiences and emotions, we offer a balanced view of this historic event.

In "Experiences of Fear, Survival, and Trauma," we provide a captivating and comprehensive analysis of the Entebbe rescue mission, its far-reaching implications, and the enduring impact it had on individuals, nations, and the world at large. Through the lens of personal stories, diplomatic efforts, and geopolitical context, this subchapter presents a multifaceted exploration of one of the most remarkable operations in modern history.

The Role of Ugandan Authorities and the Local Population

In the daring rescue mission at Entebbe, the role of Ugandan authorities and the local population cannot be overlooked. Their actions and choices played a significant part in shaping the outcome of this historic event.

Initially, the hijacking of Air France Flight 139 by the Popular Front for the Liberation of Palestine - External Operations (PFLP-EO) took place with the assistance of Ugandan President Idi Amin. Amin, known for his anti-Israel stance, saw an opportunity to align himself with the Palestinian cause and gain international recognition. He provided the hijackers with support and allowed them to use the airport at Entebbe as their base.

The local Ugandan population was also involved, albeit indirectly, in the hijacking and captivity of the Israeli passengers. While some locals sympathized with the plight of the Palestinians and supported Amin's decision, others were indifferent or fearful of repercussions. However, it is important to note that there were also Ugandans who risked their lives to help the hostages. These brave individuals provided vital information to the Israeli intelligence agency, Mossad, about the layout of the airport and the whereabouts of the hostages.

As the rescue mission unfolded, the Ugandan authorities found themselves caught in a complex web of international politics. While Amin initially supported the hijackers, he soon realized the gravity of the situation and the potential consequences. The Israeli military's audacious plan to rescue their citizens put Amin in a precarious position. He had to navigate between his initial support for the hijackers and the need to maintain his international alliances.

The actions of the Ugandan authorities during the rescue mission varied. Some officials, driven by self-interest or fear, cooperated with the Israeli military, providing them with crucial information and facilitating their operations. Others, however, remained loyal to the hijackers and actively hindered the rescue efforts.

The local population's perspective on the events at Entebbe was diverse. Many Ugandans were caught in the crossfire between the Israeli military and the hijackers, with their lives and livelihoods disrupted. The stories of the Ugandan hostages shed light on their experiences during this traumatic event and offer a unique perspective on the unfolding events.

Understanding the role of Ugandan authorities and the local population is crucial in comprehending the complexities of the Entebbe rescue mission. Their actions and choices, influenced by political motivations, fear, and personal beliefs, shaped the outcome of this daring operation. The interaction between the Israeli military and the Ugandan authorities, as well as the impact on the local population, provides a fascinating insight into the geopolitical implications and historical context of this historic event.

The Long-Term Effects on the Lives of the Hostages

"The Long-Term Effects on the Lives of the Hostages"

The Entebbe rescue mission, a daring operation executed by the Israeli military in 1976, left an indelible mark on the lives of the hostages involved. In this subchapter, we delve into the profound and lasting impact this event had on their lives, as well as the wider implications for Israeli society, counterterrorism strategies, and the perception of the operation on an international scale.

For the Israeli passengers who endured a week of captivity, their experiences were marked by fear, uncertainty, and resilience. Their personal stories recount the physical and psychological challenges faced during their time in captivity, offering a unique and firsthand insight into the human drama that unfolded at Entebbe. These accounts shed light on the extraordinary courage and determination displayed by the hostages and their unwavering faith in the Israeli military's ability to rescue them.

Behind the scenes, diplomatic efforts and negotiations were underway to secure the release of the hostages. These delicate negotiations, involving a range of international actors, offer a fascinating glimpse into the complex web of alliances and geopolitical considerations at play. The success of the rescue mission was not solely dependent on military prowess but also hinged on the diplomatic maneuvering behind closed doors.

The aftermath of the Entebbe rescue mission had far-reaching implications for Israeli society and national identity. The operation became a symbol of Israeli strength and resilience, bolstering national morale and pride. The audacity and success of the mission also propelled the Israeli military into the global spotlight, solidifying their reputation as an elite force capable of executing daring operations against terrorism.

Furthermore, the Entebbe rescue mission had a profound impact on counterterrorism strategies worldwide. It served as a blueprint for future hostage rescue operations, with nations around the world studying and emulating the Israeli military's tactics. The operation revolutionized the way counterterrorism was approached, emphasizing the importance of swift and decisive action in the face of such threats.

The role of Mossad, the Israeli intelligence agency, cannot be understated. Their meticulous gathering of information and strategic planning played a pivotal role in the success of the rescue mission. Their involvement highlights the vital role of intelligence agencies in combating terrorism and securing the safety of citizens.

The media coverage and public perception of the Entebbe hijacking and subsequent rescue were also significant factors in shaping the event's legacy. The extensive media coverage brought the story to the forefront of international attention, garnering support and sympathy for the hostages and the Israeli cause. This coverage further underscored the importance of international support and cooperation in the success of the operation.

Lastly, it is imperative to explore the perspective of the Ugandan hostages and their stories. Their experiences provide insight into the impact of the hijacking on their lives and shed light on the broader narrative of the events at Entebbe. Understanding their perspective is crucial in comprehending the full complexity and human toll of this historic event.

In conclusion, the long-term effects of the Entebbe rescue mission were wide-ranging and profound. From the personal stories of the hostages to the geopolitical implications and the evolution of counterterrorism strategies, this chapter offers a comprehensive examination of the lasting impact of this heroic rescue mission. Diplomats and historians alike will find invaluable insights into this pivotal moment in history and its enduring significance.

Reconciliation and Healing for the Ugandan Hostages

The Entebbe rescue mission, undertaken by the Israeli military in 1976, was a defining moment in the history of counterterrorism and international diplomacy. While much has been written about the bravery and heroism of the Israeli soldiers involved, it is equally important to shed light on the experiences of the Ugandan hostages and their journey towards reconciliation and healing.

For the Israeli passengers, the days spent in captivity were marked by fear, uncertainty, and the constant threat to their lives. Their personal stories and experiences during this harrowing period shed light on the resilience and strength of the human spirit. By sharing their testimonies, we gain a deeper understanding of the psychological toll that such an ordeal takes on individuals and the long-lasting effects it can have on their lives.

Behind the scenes, diplomatic efforts and negotiations were underway to secure the release of the hostages. These delicate negotiations involved intricate coordination between various international actors and showcased the power of diplomacy in resolving conflicts. Exploring the diplomatic strategies employed during this crisis provides valuable insights into the importance of international cooperation in times of crisis.

The impact of the Entebbe rescue mission on Israeli society and national identity cannot be understated. The successful operation not only bolstered the morale of the nation but also solidified the Israeli military's reputation as a force to be reckoned with. This event became a symbol of Israeli determination and resilience in the face of adversity, reinforcing national pride and identity.

To fully understand the historical context and geopolitical implications of the hijacking and subsequent rescue operation, it is essential to delve into the role of the Mossad, the Israeli intelligence agency. The gathering of intelligence and meticulous planning that preceded the mission highlight the crucial role played by intelligence agencies in combating terrorism.

The aftermath of the Entebbe rescue mission left a lasting impact on counterterrorism strategies worldwide. The successful operation served as a blueprint for future hostage rescue missions and prompted nations to reevaluate their approaches to combating terrorism. Examining the long-term effects of this mission allows us to understand the evolution of counterterrorism strategies in the years that followed.

International support and cooperation played a significant role in the success of the rescue mission. The unwavering support of various nations and their willingness to collaborate with Israel underscore the importance of international solidarity in the face of terror. This cooperation highlights the potential for nations to come together to tackle common threats.

The media coverage and public perception of the Entebbe hijacking and subsequent rescue were instrumental in shaping global understanding of terrorism. The extensive media coverage brought the issue of terrorism to the forefront of public consciousness, sparking conversations and debates that continue to this day. Understanding the media's role in shaping public opinion provides a valuable lens through which to analyze the impact of the Entebbe mission.

Lastly, the stories of the Ugandan hostages themselves shed light on their perspective of the events at Entebbe. Their voices are often overlooked in the larger narrative, and yet their experiences are crucial to truly understanding the complexity of the situation. Exploring their stories allows for a more comprehensive understanding of the human impact of terrorism.

In conclusion, the subchapter on reconciliation and healing for the Ugandan hostages aims to provide a well-rounded account of the Entebbe rescue mission. By examining the personal stories of the Israeli passengers, the diplomatic efforts behind the scenes, and the impact on Israeli society, as well as exploring the historical context, geopolitical implications, and long-term effects, we gain a deeper understanding of this transformative event in history. Additionally, by highlighting the role of international support, media coverage, and the stories of the Ugandan hostages themselves, we ensure a comprehensive and holistic analysis of this significant moment in time.